I0604319

Reckoning 3
Electronic Edition: Winter Solstice 2018

Reckoning 3 *is a communal effort. Editorial staff, in alphabetical order:*
Michael J. DeLuca
Danika Dinsmore
Mohammad Shafiqul Islam
Giselle K. Leeb
Johannes Punkt
Sakara Remmu
Aïcha Martine Thiam

Cover:
Fight or Flight by Stylo Starr

Reckoning Press
206 East Flint Street
Lake Orion, MI 48362
www.reckoning.press
ebook distributed by Weightless Books
printed by Book Mobile on 100% post-consumer recyled paper.

 ISSN 2474-7327
e-ISBN 978-0-9989252-4-0
ISBN 978-0-9989252-5-7

Reckoning 3
Creative Writing on Environmental Justice

Contents

Cover
Fight or Flight

Stylo Starr

Stylo Starr is a Jamaican-Canadian artist or "visual alchemist," and is known primarily for her multi-layered collage work, which has been featured on large public installations, international publications and apparel. Starr's visual investigations surround predominantly Bodies of Color and their relationship to the basic principles and elements of design, while reaffirming their agency as revered subjects of art history.

Journalist Evelyn Myrie writes: "For Starr, her work is a 'practice in revolutionary love', rejecting the lingering effects of white supremacist ideology."

Stylo unveiled her first major solo show at the Art Gallery of Hamilton alongside the works of Andy Warhol in 2017, and recently completed a residency with Hamilton, Ontario's Cotton Factory studios, continuing her explorations in collage and multimedia arts.

From the Editors

How Can I Look Up

Danika Dinsmore

for Michael J. DeLuca

How can I write you this letter

through thick smoke the sun
a red dot in the sky
I should not be able to stare into

How can I make an appointment
        with the car dealer
while mother Tahlequah takes
her tour of duty   displaying for us
hairless monkeys what the rest
of the natural world already knows

How can I take a shower
when thousands of people have poison
                                        to drink
How can I look out the window at the moon
        stroke my cat's chin
                        make my bed
How can I admire the late blue background
and mountain silhouette on the ferry heading home

How can I take a seat on a bus
hurtling toward a city of dog-walkers   businessmen
and concerned shrugs of passers-by
        it's terrible this smoke it's all terrible
I know   *it's really terrible*   *I know*   *I know*

How can I bring the sleeping children home
after a long day of amusement park

fried foot-long corndogs
How can I look up my visa bill when
our relationship with the earth
is toxic
stored now in blubber
of whales that send us warnings
and raw grief
a suffocation of sound and light
in the realm of the dead

How can I make plans with a friend
buy groceries drink tea
while we are plunging toward an inevitable
tipping point
no return
extinguishing what has been
like a comet
or a cancer
or a chapter of some future history book

when we alter landscapes lose habitat
when the world shrinks
gets hotter tighter angrier
goes hungry

How can I search for a lost coat
my favourite when
we are losing every day
pieces of our humanity
of green
of corals and bees
and owls and streams

How do I rekindle passion's poetry without falling into despair
feeling holding me there
when I exist in coffee pots lists renovations of the old
dish-washing laundry finally unpacking all my
books—
finding homes for paperwork and tools

getting on them weeds in the garden out of control
        testing recipes
        collecting that fruit before it rots on the trees

How do I do the deep work
maintain connection to that slightly
        MAD state
and go about my day   lost as I long to be

How can I sit in an alley playing drums with a Turkish immigrant
How can I breathe smoke on the shoreline while
using my cell phone as a hot spot to
send an email about a postcard for a
talk about climate change

How can I sleep?

How can I ask a friend how I can do these things when
he says
        H*ow can we anything*

My heart breaks because other hearts do not
        my heart breaks and I go on making plans
        scheduling dates
        daydreaming about getting laid
        calling out to alley cats
                to birds overhead
                to the leaves in the trees

How can I dress myself for success
        add accessories
        buy lemon tarts
        browse antique stores
        try on possible new shoes

my generation acquiesces to the inevitable
while millennials dream of Super Heroes
bursting through the screen

Somebody
do
something
do
something
I want to scream
        Let go of every device in your hands
and look up   are we going to lose
the sky   on our way to losing the sea

How can I leave space   for us
        to breathe

How can I
unbury your ears
shape a new kind of listening
to what is under our feet   and floating
still-born   (yet still hoping)
all around us   stating the obvious

How can we anything   he asks while
chopping onions and peppers
to feed his young family
in the midst of idling engines
cooked rivers
        air-conditioned ignorance
        and addiction to machines

Danika Dinsmore is a writer, world builder, spokenword artist, finder of lost things, tree whisperer, pronoiac pantheist, intersectional/eco feminist, Hufflepuff. A well-seasoned genetic mutt who has turned to activism as a means of expression and expression as a means of activism.

The Green Man

Teika Marija Smits

Olly, we know you can hear us," said Jack. "So are you coming to The Green Man, or what?"

Olly opened his eyes, put his hand to his earpiece and disconnected himself from the cloud. He sat up, the thin plastic mattress rucking up beneath him.

"It'll be fun," said Selma, "an adventure. They serve mead. Real mead."

"You're shitting me," said Olly.

"No, we are absolutely not shitting you," insisted Mohinder, his face as serious as ever.

Olly's eyes flicked over to Nate's mattress. It was empty, and for a split-second he was afraid.

Selma laughed. "Yeah, lover boy's coming. He's just gone to the loo."

Olly reddened, told them all to fuck off, and lay down again, his back to the three of them. As he reconnected to the cloud, music and updates streaming into his consciousness, he heard Jack again: "We go on Friday. When there'll be a full moon. A Green Grass Moon." Selma said something about bicycles.

Olly began to doze. And as he slipped into sleep his neural feed suddenly filled with strange images: a lime-coloured moon; blades of grass; a grinning man, his green face covered in leaves.

The next day Olly was assigned to the big house, specifically the attics. They needed to be sorted through, cleaned. Selma was to go too. As they trudged across the lifeless fields, away from the giant greenhouses in which they normally worked, Selma asked Olly if he was disappointed.

"About what?" he said.

"Bet you would've preferred to have Nate along."

Olly shrugged. "I'm happy to have whoever. It makes a change from pollinating."

"Don't lie," she said. "I can see the disappointment on your face."

Olly stayed silent and bent his head to his shoes, his eyes on the sterile mud oozing over his soles.

"Why don't you just tell him?" she persisted. "That you like him. What've you got to lose?"

"What's the point? He could be sent to other work, like, miles away from here, any day. And then I'd never see him again."

Selma smiled insinuatingly, nudged Olly. "But what about living in the here and now. And having fun?"

Olly waved his arm at the bleak mud fields. "Fun. Yeah, there's loads of that about, isn't there?"

"Which is why we should go to The Green Man."

Olly laughed sarcastically. "Yeah, right. Like going to a twentieth century pub is going to solve all our problems."

"I didn't say it would solve all our problems. Just . . . that going might be fun."

They trudged on in silence.

"So you gonna come?" Selma said.

Olly sighed. "Yeah, I'll come."

The staff at the big house weren't pleased to see them or their muddy shoes.

"Take them off. Right now!" said the housekeeper.

Olly and Selma exchanged glances, then removed their shoes, powerless to do anything about the mud dripping onto the smooth, clean flagstones.

"We don't really need you," said the housekeeper, leading them through the servants' quarters and up several flights of stairs. "We could've managed just fine, but Madam's got us busy with guests so we've no time for this sudden whim of hers." She gave a snort. "Spring cleaning!"

When they got to the dimly lit attics she reached into a

cupboard, handed them a few bin bags and a couple of long sticks with brightly coloured ruffles at the end.

Olly and Selma, round-eyed, stared at the sticks. Olly tentatively touched the ruffles.

"Feather dusters," said the housekeeper. "For dusting," she added, her face grim.

"Real feathers?" asked Olly.

"Of course!" snapped the housekeeper. "Now get on with it," she said, throwing open various doors. "You're to dust and sort through the chests of fabrics and clothes. Anything moth-eaten or irreparably damaged goes into the bin bags. To be donated to . . . ." Olly assumed she'd just stopped herself from saying "the likes of you". She cleared her throat. "Charitable causes."

She swept out of the room and descended the stairs. "I'll be back in a few hours," she called. "To check on you."

For a moment Olly and Selma just stood there, taking in the silence, the dust motes that floated in the beams of sunlight, the cool of the real wooden floorboards beneath their polyester-socked feet.

"What does she mean by moth-eaten?" said Selma.

Olly shrugged, then put his hand to the side of his head, to his earpiece, but of course he wasn't linked up to the cloud. In working hours the AI cut their connection. "Don't know," he said. "But we'll figure it out. You take that room," he said, pointing to an open door, "and I'll do this one."

"Okay," said Selma, disappearing into the other room, bin bag and duster in hand.

Olly breathed deep of the musty air, dozens of natural fragrances suddenly alive to his nose, and he smiled, for a moment happy. Of course it would've been better if Nate was here with him, instead of Selma, but he pushed away that thought and began to throw open chests, rifling through the beautiful fabrics, the feel of pure cotton on his skin a new joy.

At lunchtime the housekeeper inspected their work.

"Not bad," she conceded, sweeping a finger across one of the window sills and finding it devoid of dust. She gave them a couple of bottles of liquid food.

"After you've taken your calories get straight back to work. There's still a lot to do."

"Please, Miss, I mean Ms," said Selma, suddenly flustered. She didn't know how to address the housekeeper. "But what's moth-eaten?"

The housekeeper looked into one of the bin bags, pulled out a woollen blanket that was more holes than wool. "This is moth-eaten," she said. "There were once creatures, insects, that liked to eat natural fabrics. They would nest in wardrobes, in the fabrics, and eat the cloth, destroying the garment."

She put her hands on her hips and surveyed the room with suspicion, as though she expected dozens of moths to come flying out at her. "Well, keep at it!"

She turned on her heel and left them to their carbohydrate slurries, to their old-fashioned work.

Later that afternoon, when Olly was sorting through the last of the chests, a small, colourful object between two of the blankets caught his eye, something he'd only seen through the cloud. A bee. He gingerly picked it up, some long-dormant voice cautioning him to be careful, and lifted it closer to his eyes. It was remarkable. So intricate. He stroked it with his forefinger. And ever so soft. He wondered how long it had been there. Two decades, three? Just as he was about to call for Selma, he heard her scream. He immediately turned and ran to her, the bee falling from his hand.

"What is it?" he asked as he arrived by her side, her eyes wide, hands at her face.

"A, a . . . a thing . . . ."

Olly looked upwards to where she was pointing. There, in a high-up corner of the room, was a skeletal creature suspended in strings of dust. A spider.

Olly took a step closer. "It's an insect. Or rather, it used to be. Not sure what kind."

"It's creeping me out," she said. "Can you get rid of it for me?"

"Yeah, okay."

He took her duster, swirled it round the cobwebs; the spider dissolved into thousands of shards, sticking to the feathers of the duster. After a few seconds there was nothing left of what had been the spider's creation.

Olly handed the duster back to Selma. "Try not to freak out if you find anything else, okay? It's all gonna be dead, you know."

"I *do* know that," she said, whacking Olly with the duster. "There was just something about it. The way it looked at me."

Olly wanted to laugh but couldn't. He thought of the bee and hoped he'd be able to find it again. There'd been something about the way *it* had looked at him.

That night, when Olly and the other workers were in the dorm—most of them, like him, tuning out of reality and into the cloud—he pulled out the white square of cloth that he'd wrapped the dead bee in.

He turned to check that he was unobserved; Jack, Mo, Selma and Nate were all huddled together, most likely going over their plans for the trip to The Green Man, so he turned back to his package. He carefully unwrapped the bee, then stroked it. The bee made him feel something . . . what, he wasn't sure. In his head, he began to list some feelings: happy, joyful, sad, sorry. The cloud supplied him with more: nostalgic, wistful, bittersweet. He liked the sound of that last one. Then one more word floated into his consciousness. Hopeful.

No, thought Olly, folding the handkerchief over the bee and putting it back in his pocket. "Never that," he muttered, before tuning into his favourite social network.

Getting hold of the bikes had been the hard part.

"That bitch of an AI almost didn't let me take them," said Selma, hauling out four bikes. Olly, Mohinder, Jack and Nate helped her wheel them out of the barn.

"Only four?" said Jack.

"How about, 'Thanks, Selma,'" she retorted.

"It's just, you know, there are five of us," said Jack.

"So two of us have to share," she said. "As I said, the AI didn't like that I was taking them out after work hours."

"So what did you tell her?" asked Mohinder.

"Oh, some shit about how they were moth-eaten and needed to be aired. That got her stuck in a loop for a bit."

"So who's sharing?" said Jack.

The five of them were silent, their eyes on the bikes.

Nate started stroking the saddle of the bike he was holding. "The last time I rode a bike must've been, like, ten years ago. For some reason, Mum thought I should learn."

"Me, it was the other day," said Selma. "Back-and-forthing across the mud flats for no good reason."

"They still got you looking for grass?" Nate asked.

"Yep," she said. "Like I'm ever gonna find any. But Madam swears that she saw some a while ago, so Madam's will be done. I reckon she just likes the idea of me out there in all weathers looking at mud."

"But it's better than having no job. Only taking the minimum of bitcredits," Olly pointed out.

Selma nodded. "I know. But, hey, I like complaining. So who's sharing?"

Nate said that he wouldn't mind, and Olly quickly added that he wouldn't mind either.

"Good, that's decided," said Selma, flashing a smile at Olly and mounting a bike. "Follow me."

They cycled, haltingly, across the mudflats, some of them more confident than others (though Olly had an excuse for his wobbly progress—Nate was sitting across his handlebars). Jack kept checking into the cloud, to make sure they were going in the right direction. Selma kept up a steady commentary, asking, or rather telling, everyone how much fun they were having.

The Green Grass Moon, though not actually green, was huge, golden-coloured and close to the horizon as the sun began to set. As their muscles responded to the exercise, their skin to the feel of the warm breeze, they had to admit that yes, this was fun.

At The Green Man, a burly, bearded man covered in virtual tattoos told them to disconnect themselves. "We're free-range here," he explained, holding out his hand for their earpieces.

Selma pointedly stared at his shimmering, roving tattoos, and then at the sliver of metal above his ear.

The man crossed his arms, stared back.

"Turn yourselves off or you ain't coming in."

Mohinder nudged Selma. "Look," he muttered, "we didn't come all this way to get told to shove off."

Mo made a show of disconnecting from the cloud, and handed his earpiece to the bouncer. They all did the same.

"You're buying the first round," Selma said to Mo as the bouncer stepped aside and allowed them entry.

"No problem," said Mo, grinning. "Me," he went on, rubbing his thumb against his forefingers, "I'm rolling in bitcredits."

"Is that what I think it is?" asked Nate, when they'd got their first round of mead and taken their seats at a wooden booth.

"What's what you think it is?" said Jack.

Nate inclined his head to the fireplace. "A real log fire."

They all turned their heads to look.

"Looks real," said Selma.

"But think about the cost," said Nate, taking a sip of his mead. "God this tastes good."

They all began to drink; in the silence that followed they experienced a taste of spring—apple blossom, heather, primulas, daffodils, bluebells.

Selma glugged back her pint, then began to giggle. "This is just too weird. And good."

"Steady on, Sel," said Jack, "otherwise you'll be pissed in no time."

"Maybe I want to get pissed!" she retorted. "Who wants another pint?" She quickly stood, then put her hand to her head and sat back down again.

"Take it easy," said Mo. "Jack'll get the next round in. When we're all done, right?"

"Yes, boss!" said Jack, giving him a mock salute.

"Fuck you," said Mo, taking another swig, his eyes on Jack who was also knocking back his mead.

For a moment there was an uneasy silence.

"Me," said Nate, trying to diffuse the tension, "I'm just gonna savour this pint. It's absolutely delushious."

Selma laughed. "Delushious," she said. "I like that." She slurred "delushious" over and over, and they all laughed.

It was then that Olly noticed the strange man at the bar. He put his hand to where his earpiece would usually be, thinking that the image had come from his feed, then realized that the grinning green man with leaves all over his face was, in fact, real. Olly lowered his head and spoke under his breath. "That weird guy's watching us."

Selma immediately raised her head to look.

"Don't!" hissed Olly, pulling at her arm.

"You're right," Selma said slowly. "He is."

Jack, Mo and Nate surreptitiously flicked their eyes over.

"Cool skin," said Nate.

"I don't know," said Selma. "Green's a bit last season. Madam's wearing this gorgeous powder pink skin at the moment. And she's always bang on trend. When I earn enough bitcredits I'm getting myself a turquoise skin. What do you think, Jack?" she said, giving him a nudge. "Will you still lurve me?" she slurred, somewhat sarcastically.

Jack ignored her, drank some more.

"But what's with the stuff on his face?" asked Nate.

Mo shrugged. "Enhancements. Virtual markings. Disease." Mo suddenly laughed. "Maybe he's an alien. Who knows?"

Olly was just about to tell them that he'd seen this man before—either in his dreams, or in his feed—when Jack finished his pint and got up. "Right," he said, "I'm going to the bar."

"Me too," said Selma. "Actually, I need the loo."

"So do I," said Mo. "Here," he said, helping her up. "I'll take you."

Selma grinned at Olly as she left the booth. "We'll leave you two lover boys to it, shall we?"

Olly reddened, bowed his head, but Nate simply laughed good-naturedly.

When they'd gone, Nate and Olly were silent for a bit. Olly tried desperately to think of something to say. He then remembered the bee. Taking the handkerchief out of his pocket, he told Nate that he wanted to show him something.

"What is it?" asked Nate as Olly unfolded the thin square of cloth.

"A bee," said Olly, triumphant.

"Whoa!" said Nate. "That's like ridiculous!"

"I know," said Olly. "I found it in Madam's attic. Must've been there for ages."

Olly began to stroke the bee, then risked looking up into Nate's blue eyes, which were disquietingly close. "Isn't it beautiful?" He wanted to tell Nate that he was beautiful too.

Nate agreed, yes, it was beautiful. And amazing. "But just think," he went on, "if bees ever came back to Earth, we'd be out of work, wouldn't we?"

Olly, feeling rebuffed, covered the bee up again. "It's not the bees who are the bad guys here, Nate. It's those fucking miniature drones that are going to put us out of work. Or voluntary labour. The acquisition of bitcredits. Whatever the fuck you want to call what we're doing."

Olly put the bee back in his pocket.

"I'm sorry," said Nate, putting a hand on Olly's arm. "It was just an observation. The bee really is amazing."

Jack returned from the bar, interrupting them with the announcement that they served chips. "Great big fat steaming chips," he said. "Made from real potatoes. D'you want some?"

"Yeah," said Nate. "That would be–"

"Delushious," said Olly, with a laugh.

They continued to drink and make merry, and when Olly felt Nate's hand on his thigh, he could honestly say to Selma that yes, this was the best pub in the world. And that he was having the most fun he'd had in, like, forever.

When it was Olly's turn to get a round in, he found himself standing next to the strange, green man at the bar.

The man smiled at him. "Having a good time?" he said, his accent strange.

Olly nodded. "Yeah. We heard about the mead, how amazing it was and–"

"Where you from?" asked the man.

Olly, too drunk by now to worry about what he disclosed to a stranger, told him that they were from the nearby farm.

The stranger looked confused. "What kind of farm? What do you do there?"

"We pollinate the flowers of apple trees. And the other fruit trees and bushes. We spend most of our days under glass, dabbing at blossoms with a paint brush."

"That's good work you've got there," said the man. "To be amongst apple trees, the clean air that surrounds them . . . ." The man took a swig from his pint, then smiled. "Handling pollen, the very essence of life. Good work."

Olly couldn't help but stare at the strange enhancements on the man's face. They really were incredibly life-like—like real leaves. And there were also some—what were they?—acorns amongst the leaves. Before he could help himself he asked the man where he was from.

"Not from here," he replied. "But from time to time I like to drop by. I noticed the sterility, the barren soil, and thought I'd stop. Tell me," he went on, "how long has the Earth been like this?"

If Olly had been more sober he would've laughed, asked the man what planet he'd been living on. Instead he said that it had been like this for most of his life. "About twenty-five years."

"And what do you young folk think about it?" The green man inclined his head to the table at which his friends were sitting.

Olly shook his head. "We don't want it to be like this. But I guess we feel . . . " He sighed. "Powerless."

The green man nodded. "I see. So the situation's hopeless?"

"The scientists are working on it. Or so we're always being told. But I reckon that the people at the top of the food chain, people like Madam, I mean, don't give a shit. So nothing'll happen."

The man fixed his green eyes on Olly. "Do *you* think the situation's hopeless?"

Olly thought of the bee, and the words his neural feed had thrown up the other day: nostalgic, wistful, bittersweet. Hopeful.

Tears came to his eyes, and embarrassed, he hung his head. He didn't know how to answer.

"All right, son," said the man, putting his hand on Olly's shoulder. "It's going to be all right."

The five of them left the pub in the early hours of the morning, just as the sun was beginning to rise. They cycled across the mudflats, making slow, wobbly progress, the only sound the drone of driverless cars in the distance. They laughed and sang and talked about the mead, the chips, the tobacco smoke, the folk band that had rocked up to play some ancient tunes. The oldies who had danced, and persuaded them to dance.

"Delushious," said Selma, "it was all so delushious." The strange, green man was forgotten.

Suddenly, Olly stopped cycling, propelling Nate off the handlebars. "Oh God, sorry, Nate. I'm so sorry," he said, helping him up. Nate, more surprised than hurt, told him not to worry. The others slowed and then stopped.

"It's just . . . ." Olly pointed over to the east. There was the green man on the horizon, striding towards the rising sun. He seemed to be getting taller with each step.

"That's the green guy," said Jack. "From the pub. What the hell's he up to?"

Olly shook his head. "No idea."

The green man stopped, turned to face them, plucked an acorn from his face and then knelt, plunging the acorn into the soil.

The five of them felt a tremor, as though the Earth itself was sighing with relief. And then came the small noises—the squeaks and murmurings and gurgles of life returning to the soil. The green man rose, gave them a smile and then turned his back. He continued to walk towards the sun, then vanished into the first rays of light.

Nobody spoke. Nobody moved. In time, they each mounted their bikes and rode back to the farm, too exhausted, too awe-struck to speak. And as they returned to their dorm, to slip into sleep, Olly knew that they had witnessed the beginning of something new.

Outside, grass began to grow.

Teika Marija Smits is a mother, writer, artist and editor. Her writing has appeared in various places including *Mslexia*, *Shoreline of Infinity*, *Brittle Star*, *Strix*, *LossLit* and *Literary Mama*. When she's not busy with her children, or creating, she's busy managing the UK-based indie press, Mother's Milk Books. She is continually delighted by the fact that Teika means 'fairy tale' in Latvian. She can be found at: https://marijasmits.wordpress.com and on Twitter at: https://twitter.com/MarijaSmits

Endurance

Thomas Wharton

Indicators

On New Year's Eve, in small towns throughout Kentucky and Louisiana, people celebrate as they always do by setting off fireworks. The eruption of noise and light startles flocks of blackbirds, which rise up into the tumult and quickly become disoriented. While the people below dance and sing and embrace, the birds, mostly unseen in the darkness, fly into electrical wires, water towers, and the sides of buildings, while others turn on one another in the frenzy, or are attacked by other, larger birds of prey. The fireworks go on longer than usual this year, as a need has been felt for a more than usually grand spectacle of hope and renewal, and so the avian panic does not dissipate quickly but spreads to other flocks and other species of birds, up and down the countryside.

The next morning hundreds of birds are found dead in the meadows and on the highways and streets. Still more continue to fall lifeless from the skies during the day in exhaustion. People in the area, not knowing the cause, are baffled and disturbed. Many are convinced it is an omen, or at least a sign, though of what exactly, none can agree.

Forerunners

From *Wayfarers in the Libyan Desert*, by Frances Gordon Alexander, 1912

> "The Bedouin came originally from Arabia. Now he is a wanderer in the great Sahara, Libyan, Syrian, and Arabian deserts. A tribe will number from 3000 to 100,000 people, all owning camels, sheep, and goats. When it moves, the tribe sweeps over

> great tracts of country, forcing before it wolves, jackals, gazelles, and all the wild creature of the desert. The approach of these animals will often warn a tribe that another is advancing . . . ."

In our time very few Bedouin still follow their traditional nomadic lifestyle. Most of the animals are gone, too.

Duration

For the animal, happiness consists in enjoying life in the immediate present —not in the assurance that there is a whole future of joys ahead of him.

—Alan Watts

They can tell me the attack is in the past, but it isn't.

—Patricia Van Tighem

The woman is on a Sunday afternoon hike with her husband, near the town of Jasper in the Canadian Rockies, when without warning two grizzlies suddenly burst out of the thick undergrowth in front of them.

During the attack there is scarcely time for fear, and no pain, as if this is happening to someone else and she is merely there to witness it, more spectator than participant. One detail alone remains alive in her, a sensation lasting only a moment, but even now, many years after the bears broke off their attack and disappeared back into the bush, leaving the woman and her husband clawed and bruised but alive, it is a moment that has never quite ended.

As she falls to the ground with the great mass of the bear on top of her, she reaches up to ward off the onslaught of claws and teeth and her outstretched hands sink deep into the grizzly's fur. It is the softest, most beautiful thing she has ever felt in her life.

Israel and Palestine Share a Rapidly Disappearing Gazelle

—headline from *Scientific American Online*, September 11, 2015

Role Play

We are the animals who talk the fables
in which the animals talk. We are talking
animals, claiming that animals don't talk.

—Robert Kroetsch

In her biography of her husband Richard Burton, the famous Victorian explorer and translator of *The Arabian Nights,* Isabel Burton mentions an incident that occurred early in Burton's career, while he was stationed as an officer of the British East India Company in northern India:

"...he at one time got rather tired of the daily Mess, and living with men, and he thought he should like to learn the manners, customs, and habits of monkeys, so he collected forty monkeys of all kinds of ages, races, species, and he lived with them, and he used to call them by different offices. He had his doctor, his chaplain, his secretary, his aide-de-camp, his agent, and one tiny one, a very pretty, small, silky-looking monkey, he used to call his wife, and put pearls in her ears. His great amusement was to keep a kind of refectory for them, where they sat down on chairs at meals, and the servants waited on them, and each had its bowl and plate, with the food and drinks proper for them. He sat at the head of the table, and the pretty little monkey sat by him in a high baby's chair, with a little bar before it. He had a little whip on the table, with which he used to keep them in order when they had bad manners, which did sometimes occur, as they frequently used to get jealous of the little monkey, and try to claw her. He did this for the sake of doing

what Mr. Garner is now doing, that of ascertaining and studying the language of monkeys, so that he used regularly to talk to them, and pronounce their sounds afterwards, til he and the monkeys at last got quite to understand each other. He obtained as many as sixty words, I think twenty more than Mr. Garner—that is, leading words, and he wrote them down and formed a vocabulary, meaning to pursue his studies at some future time. Mr. Garner has now the advantage of phonographs, and all sorts of appliances. Had Richard been alive, he could have helped him greatly. Unfortunately his monkey vocabulary was burnt in Grindlay's warehouse fire, where his papers were in storage."
—from *The Life of Captain Richard F Burton,* by Isabel Burton, 1893

Above the Falls

The elephant has the following attribute: when he falls down he is unable to rise again.
—from the anonymous bestiary *Physiologus*, 3rd century AD

in falling he seemed for a moment to rise
— George Orwell, "Shooting an Elephant"

Someone shouts, There's an elephant in the river!

Tourists lounging sleepily on the hotel terrace after a dinner of sizzling kudu or wild boar cutlets leap out of their chairs with newfound energy. They hurry in a crowd across the sloping, well-manicured lawn to the shore, some still carrying their sundowner cocktails.

And there it is. The elephant is struggling to find a safe passage across the rushing Zambezi, only a few hundred yards above the cloud and thunder of Victoria Falls, the greatest cataract in Africa.

The elephant is attempting to cross from Zimbabwe to Zambia, the river marking the border here between the two countries. Its goal is most likely to elude poachers that have increased in number during the last few years of social breakdown and economic hardship (gunshots from the Zimbabwean side are a common sound here lately, one of the few noises that can rise above the ever-present roar of the falls). Two smaller, younger elephants wait on the shore for the older, more experienced elephant to find safe passage. This is an immemorial elephant fording place, but the river is higher and the current stronger than it has been in years. And on the Zambian side a brand-new five-star hotel has been built on a formerly much-traveled wildlife corridor, so that animals seeking to cross are forced to try less familiar, more risky channels.

While guests, staff, and wildlife officers gather on the hotel grounds to watch, the elephant struggles, flounders, finds a secure foothold and loses it again, gets swept into the current and battles his way back from the brink. People take pictures, shout encouragement, weep, angrily declare that someone has to do something. Whenever it can clear water from its trunk, the elephant calls to its fellows waiting on the shore, a shrill, exhausted bellow, more a scream, that they answer with their own cries. He may be warning them to keep out of the river. Or letting them know he's still here, that he hasn't given up yet. No one knows for sure.

The elephant makes it as far as the last rocky islet before the Zambian shore, and plunges into the final channel that will bring it to safety. But the long struggle has taken too great a toll. The elephant has no strength left to fight the current. While the onlookers watch in horror it is swept helplessly over the main part of the falls, plunging four hundred feet into the churning chaos known as the Boiling Pot.

Days later the elephant's carcass is found downstream, washed up on the Zimbabwean side and stripped of its ivory tusks.

Cull

If I were a pig I would opt for gas.

—Arnon Grunberg

A transport truck carrying pigs was involved in an accident while on the way to a pork processing plant in Burlington, Ontario. The crash occurred close enough to the entrance of the plant that employees were quickly on hand to help bring the surviving animals safely out of the wreckage. Of the 180 pigs in the truck, 138 were rescued terrified but unharmed. They were then herded into the plant for slaughter.

There are no reports that the brief disruption to the processing schedule of this one plant caused any significant delay in the arrival of bacon on breakfasters' plates.

Harambe

The meme was first expressed on May 28th, 2016, and demonstrated a remarkable evolution in only a few short weeks, mutating into new and surprising forms that few if any observers could have predicted. In the final months of the year the meme's proliferation and dispersal slowed considerably, as other sensational events captured the internet's fleeting attention, but experts predict Harambe may go on replicating itself virtually forever.

After the gorilla was shot, zookeepers hurried to the body, made an incision in the scrotum, and extracted sperm that is now being preserved in a "frozen zoo."

There's a future, the zoo's director declared in a press conference. *It's not the end of his gene pool.*

Camouflage

The killer strikes most often in the early evening. It waits at the edge of small villages, in the shadows and tall grass, for children. They come to play, or to relieve themselves, sometimes alone and sometimes in groups. When there is more than one child, the killer will usually target the youngest and smallest. Bursting out of its concealment it snatches the child in its jaws, then bounds away into the dark. Sometimes clothing, a limb, a head, is later found. Sometimes nothing at all.

From 1996 to 1997 the central Uttar Pradesh region of northern India is terrorized by a series of wolf attacks. In one year more than seventy children are killed or injured.

Because there is never more than one attack on a single day, and the same village is never attacked twice, conservationists surmise that the attacks have to be the work of a single wolf pack roaming from village to village in this small, densely populated region, carefully avoiding places where they have already hunted human prey. There are estimated to be fewer than two thousand Indian gray wolves (*Canis indica*), giving the species an endangered status comparable to that of the Bengal tiger. Nowhere else in the world do wolves and such numbers of people coexist in close proximity. This may have disrupted the natural instinct of these wolves to avoid human beings and caused them to begin stalking humans for food.

In the face of such selective, widespread, persistent terror, not everyone believes the killer to be a mere animal in search of a meal. When a boy named Anand is taken near the village of Banbirpur, his ten-year-old sister Sita Devi witnesses the event and later tells her story. She describes how the wolf came slinking through the tall grass on all fours, but then, when it had pounced on her little brother, it rose up on two legs like a man. *It threw Anand over its shoulder and ran away*, the girl tells her fellow villagers through her tears. *It was wearing a black coat, and a helmet and goggles.*

Eyewitness accounts like Sita Devi's fuel fears that the attacks are the work of werewolves, a belief passed down through millennia in tales about such creatures. Others dismiss this as folklore and argue instead that the attackers must be men disguised in wolf pelts, most likely "infiltrators" from Pakistan, India's hated enemy.

Fugitive

Now that they have gone it is their endurance we miss.

—John Berger

In 1934 a female black panther escapes from the Zürich Tiergarten and survives through two months of a Swiss winter, before being shot for food by an itinerant laborer in the mountains near Saint Gallen.

The animal's escape and disappearance quickly become sensational news. During the time the panther is at large, the authorities receive hundreds of reports from people claiming to have glimpsed the fugitive, some from the most far-flung corners of the country and beyond. There is never a confirmed sighting. Suspicious tracks in the snow always turn out to be those of dogs.

A certain religious sect asserts that the panther is demonic and should be exorcized by a pastor from their church. A clairvoyant from Paris travels to Zürich and offers her help to the searchers, claiming she's had a vision of the panther hiding in a cave of ice high up on a glacier. The clairvoyant is politely asked to return home.

The panther survives by way of her instinctual stealth and her learned distrust of human beings. She hunts mice, voles, and hares in the snow-mantled forest, as far from human habitation as possible, and makes herself a den under the roots of an ancient stone pine, from which she emerges only when hunger drives her.

One evening the panther comes upon two ravens perched on a dead fir tree, croaking softly to each other. The panther knows from previous experience that where there are scavengers like ravens, there are likely to be people. Her time in captivity has does nothing to lessen her innate distrust of humans, but where they are there is always food.

A squirrel in a nearby tree is chattering at the ravens, scolding them or perhaps even mocking their harsh voices. The birds are doing their best to ignore the squirrel and carry on their own conversation. The panther has come upon the scene from a direction that conceals her presence from the other animals. She is famished, having had no luck catching anything to eat for three days.

The squirrel suddenly darts part of the way down the tree's

trunk and freezes there, watching the ravens to see what they will do. The squirrel's perch is now close enough to the ground that the panther might possibly reach it with a quick pounce. She steals up on her prey from behind, but the ravens see her. They halt their banter at the unaccountable sight of this strange creature, and the squirrel senses danger. In an instant it has scurried back to the safety of the treetop.

The panther leaves the ravens squawking about this unexpected turn of events and prowls on, further down the mountain, finding her way at last to a small graveyard ringed by trees. Hunkered in the concealment of a thorn bush at the edge of the burial ground she can smell dead human. Eating things she has not killed herself is not in her nature, but surviving is. Still, she must be careful. She remembers how the humans first caught her. How they had a thing made of wrong-smelling vines that fell on her so that she couldn't get away. She has been boxed up, shackled, whipped. She will not move until she is certain there is no hidden danger here.

The panther waits. Humans come. There are many of them, some carrying a thing made of pieces of tree. They carry the thing to a hole in the ground. They set it down. One of them utters that strange flat barking that only humans make. Some make other noises, like the cries and whimpers the panther heard from other caged creatures around her in the place the humans kept her before she escaped.

After a short time most of the humans leave. Two stay behind and cover the hole with earth. Then they leave, too.

The panther waits until it is well past dark and then she pads silently into the burial ground. She reaches the fresh grave and slowly, with many pauses to listen, digs away the loose soil. She claws and bites at the flimsy thing made of wood and two of its pieces move apart and now she can get at what's inside. The panther hauls it out and drags it to her hiding place to eat. The dead human is small. It was weak and sickly, the panther knows when she tastes its flesh, which is dry and joyless fare. But it will sustain her.

Later a fall of large wet snowflakes patter softly on the bare branches, on the panther's fur, on the damp earth. The panther has rested after her meal, and now, in the grey light just before morning, she moves on.

Here she is now, a dark shape against the snow. We can only glimpse her from our thicket of language, at the edge of a great silence. If we come any closer she slips away, disappearing into the white page.

Ecophage

1558: Aboard the ship bringing French explorer Jean de Léry home from Brazil, the "Land of Parrots", an eerie silence prevails. All through the voyage the crowded decks have resounded with the calls, grunts, hoots, and seasick whimpers of the exotic New World animals de Léry has collected and that he hopes to present as gifts to noble patrons upon his return. But the ship has run into punishing storms and strayed into unknown waters, and with food running out and starvation looming, the crew turns at last to de Léry's menagerie for salvation. One after another into the cooking pot go monkeys, lizards, birds, and other creatures with no names as yet in the tongues of civilized men.

The explorer manages to keep his most cherished specimen alive and hidden from the crew for several days, but at last he is forced to surrender a magnificently-plumed parrot, as big as a goose, that "uttered words freely like a man."

Giddy with hunger, de Léry imagines Noah and his family on the ark, out of provisions and deciding which of the animals will be sacrificed to save the last remnant of humanity. The ones they chose struck forever from the roll of God's creation. The guoto. The malabee. The speckled orotain.

Five days later the lookout sights land. The decks resound again as the men cry to the heavens in thanks for their deliverance.

Extinction

Some words for animals in languages that no longer have native speakers:

fish, Ubykh: psa
fox, Woccon: Tauh-he
mouse, Thracian: argilos
worm, Anglo-Norman: achée
turtle, Kansa: ke
cattle, Norn: kye
hummingbird, Taino: colibri
wolf, Old English: wulf
lion, Vaal-Orange: !hoeti
buffalo, Chinook: moos-moos
horse, Phoenician: ss
dog, Mbabaram: dog

Abundance

When the last tiger is gone we all get to be tigers.

As wild animals vanish from the physical world, they have begun to proliferate in the digital realm. The videogame *Grand Theft Auto V* contains more animals than any previous version of the popular title. Among the animals one may encounter while stealing and murdering one's way through the game's fantasy of consequence-free mayhem are dogs, cats, monkeys, chickens, cows, pigs, rabbits, rats, hawks, pigeons, crows, seagulls, butterflies, houseflies, fireflies, cockroaches, snakes, voles, coyotes, wild boar, mountain lions, elk, deer, various species of fish, dolphins, humpback whales, sharks, stingrays, and even, it is rumoured, a sasquatch.

Curiously, there are no horses.

Most of the wild animals players encounter will run away at the approach of a human. On one of the game's missions players can hunt deer and other animals in the mountains outside the city and earn money for each kill. Players can also just kill animals without incentive, shooting them, bludgeoning them, or running them down with vehicles, as a diversion from the game's other brutal amusements. Every so often predators such as mountain lions turn the tables on a player who ventures into the wilderness. It is also possible for your game avatar to consume peyote plants and enter a psychedelically colourful hallucinatory state in which they *become* an animal. When they find themselves in an animal body the game's three protagonists, Franklin, Michael, and Trevor (who may or may not be a cannibal), will babble to themselves in stunned, stoned amazement at what they are experiencing:

Damn. I ain't never had no antlers before....

I'm a wild boar! I'm a badass wild boar!

Is this happening? This is happening. Shit, look at me. Does everyone become a dolphin?

Oh man, I feel weird. What is this...? Oh. Oh my lord. Hey. This is amazing! Wow. Look at you, Trevor. Look at you. No one is laughing at you now. No one. They're all losers, and you're a crow. A fucking crow. Hah! Whoo! Okay, let's party! Flying...flying.... Oh, Trevor. Oh wow. Look at your beak. Great! Look at your black wings. Great! You're amazing! This is the future...this is evolution. Man-crow! What's a man? No idea. An idiot? Yes, a man is an idiot. You're not an idiot, you're a crow. Oh wow. Haw haw. Yesssss. This beats eating policemen any day.

The Cliff's Edge

Inside the egg the heron dreams of flight

—Mirabai

The great auk (*Pinguinus impennis*) is driven to extinction in the modern era by Europeans who hunt and kill the bird for its down, used to make pillows. The bird's demise is hastened further by its own increasing rarity, as museums and collectors are willing to pay enticing sums for specimens, money that proves irresistible to poor fishers and sheepherders.

The very last colony of great auks survives until the middle of the nineteenth century, on the nearly-inaccessible island of Eldey, off the coast of Iceland. On July 3rd, 1844, three men sent in search of great auks by a wealthy collector find what is possibly the very last breeding pair of great auks in the world, incubating a single egg. One of the men, Sigurður Ísleifsson, later described what took place.

The rocks were covered with blackbirds and then we saw the geirfugles (the auks)... They walked slowly. Jón Brandsson crept up with his arms open. The bird that Jón got went into a corner but mine was going to the edge of the cliff. It walked like a man... but moved its feet quickly. I caught it close to the edge, a precipice many fathoms deep. Its wings lay close to the sides, not hanging out. I took him by the neck and he flapped his wings. He made no cry. I strangled him.

The third man, Ketil Ketilsson, finds the nest and, acting on a familiar human impulse which has yet to be fully understood, smashes the egg with his boot. That night, he and his companions return home from their long, exhausting day and fall asleep quickly, their heads filling with phantom people and scenes that vanish into nothingness and are left unrecorded when they wake.

From now on there are no more great auk dreams.

Thomas Wharton's novels, stories, and nonfiction have been published in Canada, the US, the UK, Italy, and other countries. His first novel, *Icefields,* received the 1996 Commonwealth Writers' Prize for Best First Book in Canada and the Caribbean. His first collection of stories, *The Logogryph,* was shortlisted the International Dublin Literary Award. He has also published an eco-fiction, *Every Blade of Grass.* Wharton lives near Edmonton, Alberta and teaches creative writing.

The Extinction Gong

Crystelle Vu and Julian Oliver

The Extinction Gong is a ceremonial automaton for the Sixth Mass Extinction, the human-induced process of planet-scale biological annihilation first formally recognised by scientists in 2014. Taking the form of a large traditional 'Chao Gong', its rear face is fitted with a mechanism that beats to the rhythm of species extinction, estimated by eminent biologist E.O. Wilson to be about 27,000 losses a year, or once every 19 minutes. The significance of this figure (and those like it from other scientists) cannot be overstated: for millennia the average 'background rate' of (plant, animal and insect) species extinction has been between 1 and 5 a year, right back to the 5th Extinction that took the dinosaurs 65M years ago. Should biologists declare a new species extinct while the Extinction Gong is active it will receive an update via a 3g link and perform a special ceremony: four strikes in quick succession alongside a text-to-speech utterance of the Latin name of the species lost, resonating through the gong. Seen at its front, the Extinction Gong hangs in a large metal frame and bears the stark neo-primitivist image of the Extinction Symbol, the official mark of the Sixth Mass Extinction. Seen from the back, however, it is a work of engineering, complete with mallet, electro-magnet, audio transducer, embedded computer and 3g downlink. This diametric expresses a brutal and contradicting irony: while advances in science and technology augment the devastating impact of human endeavours over wild habitats, so are they our best means of studying and understanding it. The Extinction Gong is a 2017 project by Crystelle V u and Julian Oliver.

Crystelle Vu (@pestregards): Artist mainly focused on the greatest environmental & social challenges of our time | co-organises http://blackl.st | Earthling.

Julian Oliver is a New Zealander, Critical Engineer and artist based in Berlin. His work and lectures have been presented at many museums, galleries, international electronic-art events and conferences, including the Tate Modern, Transmediale, the Chaos Computer Congress, Ars Electronica, FILE and the Japan Media Arts Festival. Julian has received several awards, most notably the distinguished Golden Nica at Prix Ars Electronica 2011 for the project Newstweek (with Daniil Vasiliev). He is the co-author of the Critical Engineering Manifesto and co-founder of Crypto Party in Berlin, who's shared studio Weise7 hosted the first three crypto-parties worldwide. He is also the co-founder of BLACKLIST, a screening and panel series focused on the primary existential threats of our time.

Tiger

Joe M. McDermott

As a one-star Inspector General for the UN's military police, I was uniquely positioned to assign myself any case that I chose, particularly after many years of hard assignments. I had chosen the matter of the mysterious Doolittle, a sort of multi-national guerrilla artist whose work I had encountered in my time amid the water riots of Bangladesh. The machines were dangerous, like wild animals.

I was following leads among machinists and fine artists in my region to no solution, limited by my own budget and time constraints, perfectly happy to find nothing at all until I retired and the case was old and forgotten, when I was suddenly assigned a powerful data crawler: an AI-algorithm named Deep Thor. The case was assigned his advanced intelligence analysis for three weeks, total, which is an astonishing amount of usage with a powerful AI on such a criminally trivial matter. I had no request or desire for this assistance. Apparently, Deep Thor had found a special interest in Doolittle, independently, and requested this deep dive to assist in case of terrorist escalation that was, I had to admit, possible given the machines' high-level industrial design and the integrated radical political manifestos. I felt I was to blame. This was a result of my own official reporting intended to justify my long-continued investigations, fed back to me by machines incapable of human nuance.

I met Deep Thor's keepers in my office in Belgium, a man and a woman. I showed them the tiger, with the bullet wound. The woman, Palakh, would be the special counsel in charge of the investigation as long as Deep Thor was on the case—my superior. She was from England, Oxford and Cambridge. She held out a naked hand, her wrist wrapped in henna, over the tiger's fur. She had the Hindi third eye permanently tattooed on her forehead. "May I touch the monstrous creation, Inspector General?" She did not need my permission, but if she would respect my expertise on the matter, I would offer her the courtesy of my honest answer.

"No," I said. "Please, gloves and only as needed. And call me Sunil. Formality is for court, not colleagues. I would prefer no one touched anything. This tiger is a robust machine, but we don't know what evidence we have yet to discover. DNA sweeps have come up negative, but new tests may be coming if Deep Thor approves of more thorough approaches."

She pulled her hand back. I appreciated the courtesy she was showing me. It was respectful. I wondered how long it would last. "My grandmother was a child among the last of the wild tigers, and told stories of them killing cattle and dogs in the hills and jungles before she moved to England. She was not sad that they were driven extinct. Her mother had terrified her with stories of tigers who took the little girls who were unable to keep up on the roads. She was not happy, either, exactly, at their loss. It was a complicated time."

"Times are always complicated. This new tiger is the source of two crimes," I said. "It killed a goat and endangered the safety of my refugees. The rhino seemed more dangerous, but the truck that hit it was found liable in court. The AI in the truck didn't respond well to unknown stimuli. It's a bit of a mess, but it's back in one of the large closets."

The other Deep Thor keeper, Jorge, kept his arms folded, appearing immune to the machine's aesthetic charms. "How was it powered?"

"There are a series of small thermal energy devices around the heat of the gears, microsolar in the eyes and a full algae diesel factory housed in a 'stomach' of sorts inside the chest cavity. That's what killed it. Bullet right into the algae."

"Like lungs?" he said. "An ecosystem inside the machine. It's hard to create that very fine balance."

"It's so elegant," said Palakh. "The machining is top quality. This was not made in someone's back shed workshop. There's more of them out there, yes?"

"We assume so. I have fifteen in custody. All different creatures, endangered and extinct. Each one is an individual, unique. The coral reef we left in place. We'll need to show them all to Deep Thor, but I'd prefer to leave it up to Deep Thor if it needs to get its hands dirty, so to speak. We have lots of data we can feed it without digging too deep into the delicate machine parts."

"Deep Thor prefers to be called 'she'," said Jorge. "She doesn't like being called 'it' or 'he'."

"Okay," I said. "I'll keep that in mind."

"Let's get started," said Palakh. "Since I can't touch anything. . . ." She pulled out the handheld that communicated to the artificial intelligence.

Deep Thor was silent as the camera looked over the robotic animals I had pulled from storage.

"Early parameters. . . ." said Jorge. "The method of powering is fascinating and complex. Suggests AI partnership. Research known AI, and look for signs of possible unknown AI. The method of production requires advanced machining. Who has the tools? The raw materials came from a source. Locate likely sources. Cross-reference with known and public records to indicate likely geographic location of original construction. Ideal outcomes: who made these? Names. Addresses. Serial Numbers."

Deep Thor didn't even ping.

"Do be a dear," Palakh added, addressing me, after Jorge's brusque command, "and investigate the usual suspects. Blogs. Terrorists groups. The elegance is immense, suggesting an advanced agent, but we must cover all our bases to stand in court. Human intuition into terrorist cells is often as effective as AI, and with your extensive background. . . ." She was the lawyer, not the programmer. She was in charge of the investigation. I was nothing more than a local liaison now, and this sounded like make-work to keep me out of the way. All my work had been handed over to machines. It was liberating, in a way. I was free to pretend this was all for the best.

"ETA?" said Jorge.

I realized he had a neuron-deep implant, so he could talk directly with Deep Thor, and had been plugged in with her to the point he was probably technically a part of her. Part of him was. How much, I would never know.

The first anyone in my precinct heard of the artist and craftsman who called themself Doolittle, a beautiful machine walked in from the jungle and slaughtered a terrified goat. It looked like a tiger. No one had seen a tiger alive in over fifty years, and there it was walking from the shadows at the edge of the refugee camp as if alive. It was a beautiful, compelling copy of a tiger with incredible details. The machine seemed to breathe and gracefully pounce. When men from the village came with sticks and machetes and a single illegal pistol, the machine saw them coming, curled over its kill and roared. It dragged the goat back into the forest and mangled the dead animal as if chewing and swallowing. But it was not a living thing. It was a machine going through the motions. When my authorities hunted it down to tranquilize it, the darts did nothing. Someone shot it. I wasn't at the scene. I don't know who fired the bullet. I never asked my men because I knew they would lie. It is not illegal to stop a dangerous machine that is not really a tiger. A living tiger would be a different matter.

It was a beautiful, decadent, terrifying work of art, and it jumped into the trees to die alone. Written on the underside of the tail, hidden under the fur, was part of a manifesto—the sort of crazed thing a madman would write about nature and artifice, and the proper memorials for all the species we destroyed.

At that time, I was part of the UN peacekeeping force preventing water riots and looting around the Bangladeshi refugee camps in the hills near Kerala. I was initially annoyed by the bother that this tiger was causing me. Some long-lost species had killed a goat and been shot. No one but the goat and the tiger were hurt; I could have spent this time seeking new water filters that were months overdue, or working the data lines to secure more recycled tin for rooftops before the monsoons. But reports on the internet about this mystery were spreading fast. It was important to keep up the appearance that the UN was maintaining order.

Then, I was taken to the machine in its elaborate glory. But for the fact that it did not bleed, from the outside, it was indistinguishable from a living, natural creature. The coat was perfect, and gelpacks under the skin gave it the impression of taut musculature. The claws were astonishing. I confiscated it as evidence of a crime, wrapped it in thick, thick, layers of UN investigative bureaucracy and sent it to Belgium for what I officially called "forensics", but was more like putting the thing in a box where no one would touch it. It would be years before anyone looked closely enough to see the manifesto underneath the tail, masked by the fur of the beast. In time, I would be able to manage a position overseeing the investigation.

Fortunately, I had no real budget, and no one took these artistic acts of public endangerment very seriously. I was sent reports and remains of other discoveries—some dangerous, some merely beautiful—and became the world's expert on the case of Doolittle. The second animal discovered, after the tiger, was a tuna fish so meticulous in its shimmering beauty, the old fisherman dragged it by knife to the boat and cut off the tail, spilling the blue ooze flotation media that mimicked powerful musculature above copper bones. After the tuna fish, a woodpecker was discovered in a place where there used to be forests. It was found out after a local scientist became fascinated with how the creature was surviving in a burned-out wasteland. It was surviving because it was a machine. More and more of these artifacts accumulated in my offices. I wrapped as much bureaucracy around them as I could. The tiger and the rhinoceros could be considered cases of criminal negligence, but the rest were merely evidence that might lead to the identity of an artist who was guilty of something no one was sure of. After I completed the mission in the Kerala, I invented the concerns about environmental terrorism: we did not know what this creator would build next, but their skill level and indifference to public safety necessitated discovery. My favorite of their works was the coral reef left in place in Australia, a hundred yards wide and drawn to full moons as if real. I got approval to dive in the night and swim among the swirling machines that danced in moonlight. There was still coral in the world, but in fishtanks only. The seas were too acid. It was like swimming in a miracle. I found no evidence, of course, nor was I truly interested in finding any.

At home, I had a 150-gallon tank in my living room, which I checked daily for proper saline composition. It was luxurious to use so much water for such a trivial purpose, but I loved to sit at night with the black lights on, the shy creatures extending out for the bits of coral food that drifted in from the feeding trays. I sipped inexpensive bourbon and thought about Deep Thor, the self-proclaimed "Doolittle" and these marvelous machines.

That night, I made a list of every known major AI, who owned them, and what access they could have to material design equipment at a high end. It was a very simple list. There are only a few dozen regulated AIs. None of them were permitted access to much more than Deep Thor's own networking access. They were permitted to talk to each other, but communications had to be typed on a keyboard or spoken into word-recognition software by their Jorge, so they could be assumed, in court, to be isolated from each other. I left them on the list. For all practical purposes, they could not have been involved in the construction of devices as anything but a guide. Still, this assumed that great and unconventional minds do not work around their own limitations.

If no extant AI had constructed these machines, it had to have been one that did not officially exist. The resources required to construct both a powerful, unlicensed AI as well as the marvelous machines would narrow down my search a great deal. After a few hours, I had a list that included a few major media conglomerates, a few military installations that I knew about, and seven major universities. I followed my intuition and scanned the faculty names against criminal databases in the global network. In the end, I selected a university with both an excellent industrial design department and a computer researcher who had been arrested on a nature preserve in his youth, then later at an environmental protest. He had joined the department five years before the first of the amazing machines was discovered. I cross-referenced his convention and travel schedule from public records and airline manifests. He had officially never left the country, but the complexity of the machines implied accomplices. I ran a comparison of the manifesto against his accessible publications and came up with a match close enough to sound impressive to anyone who did not understand the algorithm's accuracy percentages. In fact, any two people speaking the same language with similar subject matter most of the time would produce an 85% match, and my chosen suspect had written a lot about environmentalism.

I communicated to Palakh that I had a human lead and provided a brief report about my findings of his criminal record and written materials match. I informed her of my intention to travel to Alabama, to the university there. She told me that Deep Thor would handle this, that I was support staff only. I suggested that industrial design of this skill required an expert, and I wished to speak with one directly, to get a sense what cutting edge researchers in design might intuit about their own industry. *People talk to each other,* I said. *Rebellious people talk to each other more. Someone must have heard something. With his criminal record, he's an ideal human source on the field, and human sources don't talk to AI the same as they do people with impressive badges.*

I did not tell Palakh that I thought I might have already found a good candidate to be our mysterious creator, Doolittle, but I assumed Deep Thor would know my angle of investigation in milliseconds. I assumed I was being watched. My travel budget was approved.

Two days later, I was in Alabama, in the middle of winter, bundled against the light snow and wind that I found reminiscent of spring in Belgium, but it was still so unpleasant to me compared to the warm, dry winters in Kerala. I had taken with me an official government computer with a full accounting of the machines. It was disabled from networking, and shielded from most intrusions, but it would allow me to engage in materials research to address any line of questioning I might encounter.

I went to the university before I bothered with a motel or a meal. I was racing against Deep Thor. My researcher's name was Dr. Wayne Garcia, a native of Alabama and graduate of their prestigious industrial design school. His office was part of a cubicle farm in a poorly lit basement. He wasn't at his desk, but nobody stopped me from rifling through it. I found his class schedule taped to the bottom of an empty drawer. It was the only thing inside the desk drawers. There were a few books in a stack on top, all of them textbooks, a place to receive papers, and no photographs of family. It was a bleak desk, in a dusty basement full of cubicles, and seemed like the kind of place a revolutionary would radicalize. I snapped a picture of his schedule and went hunting on campus for the class he was teaching about robotic design elements for non-human spaces.

I scanned his file again while I waited for his class to end. Dr. Garcia had been one of the many Americans of his generation to receive his first degree in prison. He had driven his car into a nature preserve, illegally, with stolen computer parts in the trunk. He pled guilty, and the state arranged for him to go straight into the rehabilitation program. He graduated in three years and went from prison to a scholarship for graduate study in industrial design. From there, the only sign of his rebel youth was an arrest for disorderly conduct during an environmental protest, when the preserve where he had been arrested previously was sold off in a budget crisis. Companies don't generally hire people who rebel against companies. Nothing in his file suggested he was unhappy about that. He published his research on topics as esoteric to me as speaking raw code with Deep Thor, but it always had an angle towards reclaiming the environment we had lost, like how to pull carbon out of the air or de-acidify the oceans.

Dr. Garcia's class ended, and his students filed out. I stood in the hallway, my UN badge folded in my hand. The professor fielded questions from students eager for better grades. This was his potential workforce, of course. One man, alone, couldn't produce so many elaborate machine parts. Doolittle, whoever they were, required a workforce and access to serious automation. It was fairly simple to imagine a clever, activist professor assigning eager students extra credit work on some of the internal parts, things that wouldn't seem like anything out of context, but could become part of a complex network.

The professor was a corpulent giant with a red-tinged bald head and a bushy, black beard that bounced cheerfully while he chatted with students. He seemed happy enough. He enjoyed teaching, it appeared. Would he risk this joy over elaborate art projects no one would see? Did he even understand the legal consequences of what he was allegedly doing? He had not traveled outside of Alabama for years, so it was unlikely he had physically delivered the machines. If he could be proven to be involved, Deep Thor would need to root out his co-conspirators.

I wondered what Deep Thor was thinking, and if this was how it was thinking. Advanced AI don't think like humans. They have to learn how to think, which gives them an advantage over us. Evolution taught us how to think, but it also limited us to what helps us survive and breed. Deep Thor does not have that limitation, yet. She can teach herself to think around problems in ways we can't even imagine. Three weeks of impossible gymnastics over this minor crime would turn up any number of things.

Dr. Garcia saw me staring. I waved him over. "Is there something I can help you with, sir?" he said.

I smiled and handed him my folded badge. "Yes, Dr. Garcia," I said. "Feel free to call me Sunil. I am not one for honorifics. Perhaps we can talk somewhere in private?"

Confused, he looked at my ID, then at my face, then back down at my ID. Color left his face. "What is this about, Sunil?"

I took my ID back. "Shall we go somewhere private. Off-campus, maybe?"

"Am I in some sort of trouble?"

"Dr. Garcia, I've come a long way. Mind granting me a few minutes of your time somewhere private?"

"We can go to my office," he said.

"Please, allow me to select the location." His office was all cubicles. Anyone could come and go, listen in, interfere.

His head and face flushed deeper. He had likely never thought he would garner the attention of a high-level UN Peacekeeper. His run-ins had been with local forces only. What was a global Inspector General doing at his door? I'd learned from his schedule he had no more classes today. I had inadvertently timed my visit perfectly. Is there room for luck in an AI's mental landscape?

I took Dr. Garcia to his own house in my rented car. He led me inside without complaint. He had a small house for such a large man, cluttered, each surface occupied by part of some project or other. Nothing stood out as related to the investigation at hand, and much of it looked like student work. He kept the kind of house that indicated few people came over to his house. He moved a stack of papers off a chair and gestured for me to sit. I opened my laptop and pulled up a picture of the beautiful tiger.

"Do you know who Deep Thor is?" I said.

"No. Can I get you something to drink? Tea? Coffee? Water?"

"No, thanks. Deep Thor is one of the most powerful AIs in the world. Industrial designers, like yourself, really ought to know about Deep Thor."

"Well, I don't work a lot with AI. I'm not a game theorist. I don't do mainframes. I do extremely elaborate gears, pistons, that sort of thing."

"Deep Thor has been tasked with hunting down an international criminal. When AI is involved in finding criminals, they are found. I just want to make that clear. Deep Thor will find the criminal. Our conversation is nominally about the quest for this criminal, but the people who manage Deep Thor have urged me to accept that my role in the investigation is ceremonial at this point, and the best I can hope to do is stumble into something that helps Deep Thor move through the data even faster."

"So you're wasting my time, Inspector General Sunil Khan?"

"Just Sunil, if you please. I'm wasting my time, not yours." I scrolled to a close-up of the bullet hole, the machine parts revealed behind the skin of the tiger. His reaction was blank, at first. Then, he cocked his head and his jaw opened.

"It's beautiful," he said. I watched his face very carefully. Was this a braggart trying to hide his pride? Was this a man observing for the first time? I decided to trust that he knew nothing and that my instincts were correct. "What is it?"

"You tell me," I said.

"Well, it's got layers of complexity, for sure, and top notch construction. Did it escape from a theme park? They do stuff like that. Nothing that elaborate, but. . . . They do like their trade secrets."

"Do they? This one is dangerous. Theme parks abhor liability."

"Why is this one dangerous? Who would make something that complex and dangerous?"

"This fascinating machine has autonomous AI installed to mimic real tigers most impeccably. It killed livestock."

"Jesus," he said. "Why would someone build that?"

"An excellent question. I thought I would ask you that question. Let's say you are the creator. Why did you do it?"

"What?" He seemed genuinely surprised.

"Are you not the maker of this, or part of the team?"

"I. . . . No. No way. That's way above my league."

"You have access to all the materials through the university. You have a history of environmental activism. I compared fragments of a manifesto associated with this machine's creator to your published articles, and it matched to 85%." No court would accept 85%. Usually, I wouldn't, either. He didn't know that.

He looked down at his hands. I was surprised to see that he appeared to be acting guilty.

"I think I need a lawyer," he said.

"No," I said.

"What?"

"No, you need to know that Deep Thor will find Doolittle. I only came here for a consultation."

"I'm not Doolittle," he said.

"I believe you, but. . . . Deep Thor will find Doolittle, no doubt."

His hands were shaking. He stood up. "I'm being framed?"

"Who is framing you?"

"One of the AI. You just said so."

"I said no such thing."

He shrugged. "Does it even matter? I couldn't make that in a hundred years. It would take a team of people years to make the prototype for just one internal part. How could anyone do it in secret? People in my field, we talk to each other. We patent things. We need to make money with our machines, so we sell them. We have conventions. We get cocktails and drink too much and blab. Anyone with that level of skill would shit themselves about it with peers, wouldn't they? Whoever built this would be bragging to someone. That is a level of detail that's just. . . . I mean, I'd brag. I'd be a legend."

I nodded. I leaned back. We are guided by evolution, of course. That's why law enforcement work can catch criminals with the systems we know, independent of machine learning. Humans obey certain rules, certain patterns, even when we try not to. A creator of this calibre would talk; he was right. A team of this calibre would have too many human points of weakness.

"Deep Thor will find someone to blame," I said. "Her team is very good at guiding her to a subject."

"What do you want me to tell you, then?" he said. "Are you here to pin this on me?"

I shook my head.

"I'm going to leave this computer here with you, okay? For one night, I'm leaving this right here. Go over it. You can't legally export any files. It's secure. Law enforcement encryption. But I'm going to leave it with you for one night, open for your eyes, okay? You can see all the pictures of all the machines. You can analyze them for one night, take pictures of your own, study how they work. There's more of these out in the world. We don't know how many. I ask you again, Dr. Garcia, why would you make one of these things? You have access to facilities that could make one. Your students are a labor force that could be exploited by a clever man without their awareness. You are, I can tell, a clever man."

"I'm clever enough to know you're insane," he said. He was pale as a corpse, sweating.

"In court, Deep Thor's analysis will appear more accurate than the instincts of one old-fashioned policeman. You and I can say whatever we like. Evidence will be found, one way or another. Doolittle does not want to be caught."

"So you want me to make my own evidence to get myself framed?"

"No," I said. "Maybe. Not really. I want you to do the things that humans do."

"Shit myself because an AI is about to frame me to the UN?"

"Talk," I said. "Build out of pride. Spread this work among your peers. Patent. Brag. Build teams. Personally, I think reckless endangerment is a serious crime, but the world was more beautiful with tigers in it, don't you think? This machine killed one goat, and a man shot it knowing it could have been the very last one. Many of the others that have been found have been even more innocuous than the tiger. Still, I think the world was more beautiful when there were tigers. If you tell anyone I said that, I'll arrest you for perjury. This is a secret game we are playing against all the greater forces of the world. I am drafting you into the game, my friend."

What I was telling him settled slowly into his bones. He started to weep. He was afraid of me, of what I represented, and of being arrested again. This giant was afraid of me. I had seen it before, and it always felt out of place. It was a natural response to the will of the state, an unknown and unknowable as any AI entity. I am glad no one else was there to see. I touched his hand. "It's going to be okay," I said. This was not true. There were no coral in the oceans, no great nature preserves, no tigers, no bluefin tuna, no rhinos in Africa. The best any of us could do was design machines that copied them and preserve what still hung on in cages and aquaria. Nothing was going to be okay for any of us. "What was the name of your nature reserve, Dr. Garcia?"

"Talladega," he said. "It used to be a huge national forest, but the government sold it off piece by piece until it was just a reserve. It was the most beautiful place in the world. People need housing, I guess. They need minerals and lumber and land."

"I grow coral," I said. "We all do what we can."

I moved the computer to a table closer to him. He was rocking and holding himself. "Okay, I think I'm in. Yeah. Okay. What do you want me to do, Sunil?"

"I leave this here tonight," I said. "Don't take it out of your house. Do your best. I will come by in the morning, while you are in class, and I will retrieve it. Lock your door. I will have no difficulty getting in. I will not leave a mess. Don't worry about Deep Thor. She won't come after you, I promise."

He nodded, ashen. He got himself under control. I hated lying, but it helped Dr. Garcia. Honestly, I did not know what Deep Thor would do. I could never think like her. I didn't believe Deep Thor wanted a fall guy, because then the machines would stop. I believed I knew what was happening.

Dr. Garcia did as I told him to do with the computer.

I was on a flight back to Belgium by the middle of the afternoon, the next day.

Upon my return, I met with Palakh, alone. She asked after my fact-finding mission. I saw she had a networking device open. I assumed it was set to allow Deep Thor to hear me speak.

"I was able to confirm a suspicion of mine with a leading expert in the field," I said. "I may not be an AI, but I like to think I have some good instincts into the nature of man after all my training and experience in the field. Please, tell Deep Thor that I know."

"Know what?"

"Just tell her that. Tell her that I know. I want to know what she says. Deep Thor, are you listening in? I know."

We sat in the room, then. We were quiet, waiting. Palakh was confused. Deep Thor was processing and not responding, and Palakh pulled up the network energy usage data, confused.

"I see. Speechless. Tell Deep Thor something else for me," I said.

Palakh cocked her head. "I'm in the dark here, Captain."

"Tell Deep Thor that she can stop now."

That got Deep Thor's attention.

Palakh, confused, said, "She wants me to thank you," she said. "That's all she said. I look forward to reading your report."

"I will be most thorough," I said, with a most professional optimism, I must say, for such a brazen lie.

I shook Palakh's hand and waved good-bye to Jorge, who

had come out into the hall to get a look at me in passing. We shook hands briefly, looking each other in the eye with great respect, I believe. I went to the room with the machines. I packaged them back up for storage. Wrapped in layers of bureaucracy, Doolittle's astonishing machines were re-entered into legal limbo, where they would be safe for a long, long time.

Joe M. McDermott is the author of nine books, including *The Fortress at the End of Time* from Tor.com.

Eruptions

Lynne Sargent

The land knows
what we refuse to learn:

sometimes you must destroy
what has come before to create
new, unsullied things.

***

There are places my feet have trod
that are gone
never to be loved again.

The fire consumes
slowly, with enough time to flee
yet still relentless in remaking.

***

The ash like snow, blankets
the black cracked land covering
all that came before.

A goddess shows her children
the wisdom of destruction

***

The swordfern, the Ohia Lehua take
their first breaths, explore, make
a mission of re-seeding.

***

What comes next will be better,
and if not?

We burn it down again.

Lynne Sargent is a writer, aerialist, and Ph.D student at the University of Waterloo. She has been published in venues such as *Strange Horizons*, *Twisted Moon Magazine*, and *Wild Musette*, and was a 2018 Rhysling Award Nominee and 2018 Aurora Award Nominee. If you'd like to find out more about her or her work, reach out to her on Twitter @SamLynneS.

Displaced Water

Seth García

Somewhere from the diagrammatic stolon
of overgrown seagrasses, a voice carries
to the surface—*to live radical compassion,*
not just speak of it. The spiders still have not forgiven
me. The fish kill cited in the civil suit just a bead
in the course of stories scrolling by in my palm
like air pockets in rain—over 600,000 displaced
in Sri Lanka, two hundred dead and counting.
This is late May, 2017 AD. Flashbacks
of headlines some years back—
that heatwave which claimed some 2,000
in India but can this be more than read, felt
as the steadfast lamprey must feel, mooring
the stones of its own deathbed in the cool
lunar hollows? How it must feel, to prescribe
a burn, to watch the Oroville overflow with
predictions, the denial, *no more water*
in the pail! No more moon in the water!
What blame can be placed on the government
now? Someone says *relief* and means it.
Suppose blood could be set afire
with a simple question. Suppose we could
touch through the screen. Suppose speeding,
solitary, down the breathing highways
at the center of me, a course burns
its engine towards a future where hope
has long gone become obsolete.

Seth García is based in Albuquerque, New Mexico, where he is currently pursuing an MFA in poetry. He is the recipient of the North Street Collective Summer 2017 Artist Residency. His work can be found in *Slipstream*, *Zone 3*, and *Boston Accent*, among other places. He is a friend of trees.

More Sea Than Tar

Osahon Ize-Iyamu

My father thinks it's a good idea to row through these floods. To move a paddle and be above the water, finally in control of our bodies—that is to say, not drown.

But sooner or later, we're all going to fall, because we can only stand so tall before we're sinking: to our legs, to our knees, to our torsos, to our heads. Till there's nothing left and we breathe in particle dust and water that draws too much like ogbono soup. Water that's mixed with the leaves and the soil and the garbage I didn't throw away properly. Water that isn't water.

So I can indulge this feeling my father has. I can understand these spur-of-the-moment decisions when we've been waiting so long for the promise of dry land and all the water wants to do is rise.

He's always been the person with big ideas, weird reasoning. The person who suggests this over family dinner with a fire in his eyes, demands it while he paces around the room, hooked on the lust of his dreams.

"No," my brother says, pulling him back down to earth. Joseph, who helps provide for the family with Mummy, who's friends with important people. "Why would we do that?"

To our feet, to our ankles, to our ribs, to our throats . . . .

"Haven't you ever wanted an adventure out on the open sea?" My father laughs, pacing around the room. We move with him, our steps familiar as we trail the blue carpet back and forth. That's how we make the food digest.

"It's not an open sea," my mother adds before going back to her food. She never takes sides on these ideas, just points out the most clear information.

"Figuratively," my father counters, shooting her a deadpan look before returning to my brother, who folds his arms and raises an eyebrow.

"Okay, okay," my father laughs, taking a deep breath. "Facts. You just want facts. We can't drive a car in these times. Even using those suction shoes that help you stay on walls are dangerous if you lose enough friction or don't come into contact with any buildings or places you can stick yourself to. With my idea we can actually start to get more work done again, you know. Look at us, not knowing much about what goes on outside this community.... We can't live this way."

"Mummy," Joseph asks. "What do you think about all of this?"

"I think your father already has the canoe," she says, leaving her plate of unfinished food on the table, then walking up to her room.

"And," my father continues. "Once I start making money again, we could get a small ship or... you know, something more feasible."

I shrug. The rain outside makes my body run cold; I can actually hear the floods swishing all around us through our thin walls.

Thin enough for the ceiling to give out above where I stand, water splashing through. It soaks me so much that my clothes are see-through, stuck on me while my teeth chatter. Joseph runs into the kitchen to get a bucket and a mop. He cleans up and I go to my room to change into a fresh pair of clothes.

The rush of water persists and the container under the hole is half full in the minute I take to dry off and come back.

"Get up early tomorrow so we can go in the morning," my father says, scrolling through his phone, relaxing in the comfiest chair.

"Go?" I stutter, running the towel through my hair.

"Out in the open," he says, smiling with plaque-filled teeth. "I heard no objections."

I give no protests. I say no words, because when I look at all the holes in the house where the water comes through, I think that everything is falling apart, and I don't have an answer for that.

Before we go out, my mother gives us three things: coats, umbrellas, and boots. When she's not looking, I trade my umbrella for a spoon. Life's more interesting that way.

Spoons are great. I used to be obsessed with them a few years back, playing with them in all their shapes and sizes. They can be drums and help dig the soil, little wheelbarrows for transporting goods. Spoons can be everything, and they remind me of a time of no fear, only adventure. Which is what I want. What I need.

We stuff all our things in huge hiking backpacks, keeping our hands free to lift the huge canoe above our heads. I hide the spoon in my pocket.

"You won't come with us?" my father whines, frown lines unnatural to his face.

"No. My mother pushes the coat to his chest with such force that it's like she hates his presence. She walks upstairs and slams the door shut. My father fumbles around like he doesn't know what to do anymore.

"She's probably in a bad mood," Joseph says, nudging Daddy.

"Every damn day," he mutters as he opens the door for us.

Floods of water come screaming through, thick and muddy.

Outside, each step is a promise of going under, the disappearance of our bodies under muddy reflections. Each step brings back the memory of exploring the shallow far ends of our community three months ago and seeing bloated dead bodies floating in the stagnancy. Each step is running, running while the water draws me back into its thickness, running before we've even started—

I go too fast. I slip on ground that's barely solid. My head hits the water hard, breaking the surface, the impact reverberating in my skull as I go deep down under.

I can't breathe. When I open my mouth, I get the rancid taste of sickness, of cholera and dysentery, of swallowing bugs and mosquitoes. My lungs are filling up. I can't scream but only fall deeper into the dreariness, like weights are on my feet. My eyes widen; I can't blink in this space, can't do anything but die.

Strong hands pull me back to the surface and I breathe. And breathe. My chest relaxes and I vomit all the water that tried to enter me. All the disease and sickness that ever touched my tongue, the pollution and sand and *ugh.* I still don't feel right. I still can't live right.

"What the hell just happened?" My father shouts. He grabs my shoulders.

Don't touch me, I want to say, because my knees feel weak and his body weight only feels like it's pushing me down, taking me back to the deep.

"This was a bad idea," Joseph spits, shaking his head, "I think we did our best, but it's not going to work. We're already seeing bad signs."

"Nooo," my father says, holding me tighter, smiling at me, pushing the canoe to my chest like he's made my answer for me. "Just some bad balance. Uti, you still want to do it, right?"

"Sure," I say, but my brother isn't convinced, so I smile. I don't believe myself either, but I've lost my sense of adventure, my sense of wonder, and I need that back. I need this idea of fantasy, that none of this will break me, because I can't deal with it anymore. There's nothing left to sustain me but the heartbeat in my chest, so painful and incredibly fast, palpitations upon palpitations, and I need *more.*

Joseph shakes his head, then tugs my arm. "We should probably go back. I'm doing pretty well with this online business of mine, and we can just keep receiving our packages and paying our bills and—"

"And I'm doing nothing!" my father screams. The canoe falls out of his hands, its full weight going into mine.

My brother grunts, arms folded, his face turned away from us. It's eerie to watch him go limp, face slack and full of disappointment, eyes accusing. In that moment, he is exactly Mummy, and he knows my father can't handle that.

"What?" My father starts, his face folding into lines and lines of anger, veins of temper and pain. "Is it just four years in Alaska to study IT on scholarship that made you start challenging—"

I let the canoe fall so it smacks the surface of the water. It's enough to get their attention. I consider that a victory and raise my spoon to the sky like the hero I'm not, my legs shaking. "How about an adventure, guys?"

A world of obstacles lies ahead of us. Soon, we're paddling out of our neighborhood, into the depths of other roads we wouldn't dare step foot in on a normal day.

Into the mutation.

My brother starts whispering to me, clearly pissed off as he paddles. "I just think it's silly how he just led us here to sort of soothe his bruised ego and fragile mascu—"

"Let's keep going." I cut him off with a smile, rowing faster, and shift away from him. I don't want to deal with any more drama.

We enter this new place, and the smell that quickly fills our noses is a welcome, *for you have been gone so long, stayed within safe parameters, and now you are out in the big open world*; the stink becomes part of us within minutes. Makes our insides feel like they're rotting and falling apart.

But in all good adventures, it is important to leave your comfort zone, so I remind myself that this is all a journey, and in the end we go back home.

I'm grateful that I can return to a community that's not full of diseased sea creatures stalking for prey, that I stay in a place with reasonable communication and transportation services, so we can always get our food packages, pay our bills, and call our relatives. What we have right now is pretty good, is stable, is worth everything.

Other humans pass by, all of us vulnerable without solid ground.

My father, Joseph and I don't talk. We are studying this new environment, expanding our understanding with every direction we look in.

This new community is smelly yet vibrant, loud and exciting. It's what I've never seen before: vendors carrying goods on their heads with water up to their chests, chasing boats. Garbage floating around in neat little piles—some people managing to rest on top of them, the world's pollution the newest source of transportation. People breezing by on larger vehicles than ours while afrobeats, loud and violently Nigerian, play in the background. People jumping into the water with ropes tied around their waists, latched to their boats as they repeatedly bring up trash. People splash in the water as they swim through the filth and garbage, covered in boils and scars, disease and infection.

That was once me swimming, a long time ago. With innocence and purity, during floods not as bad, my little hands trailing the depths of our community, and then outside our area, with glee on my face. Carefree. Before our family locked ourselves in one place. I remember that time and I think, who was that? Not me.

But I hope to be what I once was again.

I spot a crocodile dancing in the depths, its shadow eventually rising from the surface of the water, covered in greasy film and toxic waste. Rubbish that has . . . congealed and grafted to the animal's skin—oh my goodness—like an infection sewn and healed onto the body. Like an operation done to make all living things abominations.

It passes by me with what looks like hunger in its eyes, and I know that somebody is going to die today. Someone is going to fall into its mutated jaws, and I pray it won't be me because I've already had my dance with death today and I don't plan on another.

To our toes, to our waists, to our shoulders, to our eyes . . . .

"Uti, you just might want to paddle away from the gutters," says Dad.

"Huh?" I snap out of my trance, for now.

Joseph points to the lopsided car submerged between what was once a road and the verge. People are diving around it, picking it apart.

Humans are vultures, I think, the way we decompose dead machines by taking them to bits, leaving the useless parts for the earth.

We do recycling and environmental sanitation in our community every Saturday, our part in helping to fix the world. Our elected community official praises us and tells us that by sometime in the next decade, all the trash in our area will be gone.

We may not have that long.

Till our eyes can only blink in mucus and particle dust . . . .

"Why not go near the gutters?" Joseph asks. "It's out of most people's way."

"The trash used to go in there a lot when there was land, so that it created a blockage. Plus, what lurks in there can easily kill us all," says my father.

We look down and catch the shadows we haven't noticed

before. The shadows of animals merged with glass and plastic, mosquitos breeding, insects mutated by industrial waste and chemical reactions.

My brother nods like he's actually impressed. "That's some good looking out."

My father rubs his hands and licks his lips, staring out into the wasteland in front of us. "This is what I'm talking about! We're finally out of that *community*. We were hermits and now we're reintegrating back into society. So, who's ready to get to business?"

"This boat is really . . . primitive." Joseph hits the side of the canoe and the wood groans, reminding me of the pitiful nature of our vehicle compared to the jet skis and mechanized boats, the advanced water craft that we don't have. All the things better suited to our survival. That we lack.

"Our days are numbered," I say.

They give me a concerned look, the *we need to talk about how you've become so obsessed with death* look.

But I don't want to discuss that, so I change the subject. "Yeah, let's trade."

We get home and go our separate ways. My brother goes to work. I play chess on our spotty internet service, holding the router above my head so I can stay connected to my online opponent. They win.

I trail the slow internet. I know exactly what I want to look at.

Drowning. Horror movies where people just keep getting eaten by sharks and animals.

I'd like to want to survive, but I've almost given up. If I can just desensitize myself enough, maybe it will feel less painful when the inevitable happens.

No. No. I hate the way I'm thinking so I shut my laptop to try and force myself to engage. I sneak into Mum's room but she's too engrossed in a stuttering program about unhappy marriages. She doesn't turn my way, her headphones blocking me out. I close the door.

I don't actually need to deal with that. I know I'm supposed to be there for my parents, but I can't. I need to focus on trying to stop spiralling.

So I run towards my brother's room, desperate, thinking, where's my adventure? Where's the story? Where is the actual damn plot to this movie that is my life. Because all I've been doing is running around, watching walls collapse, waiting to die.

I burst into my brother's room, drenched in sweat and breathing fast. "What are you doing?" I say.

He looks at me. "Are you all right?"

"What's that on your table?" I say. I read the brochures and blueprints on his desk. "Underwater living facilities? Oxygen suits? Enhanced deep sea living experience? Decontamination pods?"

He smiles at me and his eyes catch the light. He looks so like our father that I want to listen to what he has to say, because he's never looked this passionate about anything.

"We're looking at a hopeful future," he says. "Better opportunities, a higher standard of living; a life underwater, free of pollution—very far away from here."

"In how long?" I ask, not expecting much because it's always an estimate, always 'in a decade' and 'in the near future' and 'many years later'. Hope is never now.

"Soon. Eventually. And I can't tell you much because it's just a lot of discussing with friends who are under strict NDAs, but, yeah, they might have a space for us. It's been in the works for years. I think we'll be fine."

I'm lost for words but what kills the silence is the bleep in both our pockets. A text from Dad.

"We're going out in search of meat tomorrow," I read.

Joseph laughs. "Figures he'd try to opt out of this vegan lifestyle as fast as possible. He's looking towards the now, survival . . . which is a perspective, I guess."

Animal products haven't been transporting well, and prices have risen with the water levels, so we don't ask for them anymore. We tried fishing once but it didn't work; the fish that do come into our area are mutated. We won't eat them, won't try, no matter how adventurous Daddy is.

But since we're journeying, going out in search of things, I dream of bacon and fat running over juicy slabs of beef, the sound meat makes when it hits the pot.

We row towards the markets and vendors we saw yesterday, in the mutated areas.

We, a modest family without a proper seafaring craft, row towards a market seller, using our paddles to shove aside sticks and huge piles of rocks.

"Wetin you get?" My father starts, way too excited not to use pidgin. In our community, it's generally frowned upon, so my father only uses it when chatting with maids from the village.

The woman pauses, hands on her lips. "We get um . . . croc, jellyfish, fish worm, bongafish, catfish—"

"Catfish!" Daddy replies too quickly, reaching into his pocket, then looking uncomfortable.

"I'll pay," Joseph offers, pursing his lips as he fishes for his wallet.

"I didn't ask you to." My father's voice is cold. "We just want to examine the goods. Madam, let me see what you've got."

The woman hands over a piece of sliced catfish that's an unhealthy brown colour. It rolls in my father's hands, covered in a sticky slime. Greenish-black dots grow inside its mouth. We try to peel them off but they grow back again.

Bile rises in my throat and I almost gag.

"No, na," my father hands it back to her. "Not this one. Normal catfish wey no get all this . . . yama-yama."

"Yama-yama? Contamination?" The woman feigns surprise, like she's never heard that word when *hello? It's all around us.* "I no sell that kind product. This one, na me spice am self. I just had to preserve am well for customer."

"Thank you," my father says, irritated, and throws it back to her. He whispers to us as we leave: "All we have to do is network and we'll find someone that knows where to get good products. Someone . . . like those two!"

He points at a man and a woman collecting trash from the water, digging deep and organizing it into neat piles on their boats. The ropes around their waists are attached to the boats. My father nods in approval.

We row up to them.

Daddy puts on a smile and runs a hand through his hair. "Can you imagine? I tried to buy things from that woman and she tried to convince me that yama-yama was normal."

"They never admit it," the woman replies. "One time, you could even see all the glass and stone buried inside the fish the woman was trying to sell me, and when I showed it to her, she just doubled down and said 'all na spice.'"

"Well," the man joins in, "Nigerian hawkers are the best lawyers you could ever have."

They share a laugh while Joseph and I share a look, shrugging and folding our arms as we watch this unfold.

The man stretches out a hand to our father. "I'm Mr. Abalaka."

The woman goes in for a hug. "And I'm Mrs. Eneyo."

My father smiles. "I'm David. And these are my sons, Joseph and Uti."

We wave and greet, just enough for it not to feel uncomfortable.

Joseph shakes their hands, craning his neck to look into their boat. "That's a lot of equipment you have there."

I take a good look too. There are many weapons in their boat: spears, guns, nets, traps. I'm actually comfortable seeing all of that, because to me it screams protection, and survival.

"So, what do you guys do?" my father asks, his eyes wide like he's taking notes.

"Oh, you know," Mrs. Eneyo replies, her pleasant demeanor fading. "A lot of side-work. Helping to clear up this place, fishing work. Just . . . anything to live."

"We take our jobs very seriously," Mr. Abalaka adds.

"Oh yes," my father says. "You know, my wife does actually grow some food using spores and artificial nutrients, so we could get some for you."

Mrs. Eneyo frowns. "We already do that, but with yams and carrots and cassava, so unless you have anything else?"

"Um," my father says, trying to recall. "I think we also have garden eggs."

Mrs. Eneyo makes a face "Hmmm, I'm not—"

"But we can try them!" says Mr. Abalaka.

"Well, how much are they?" Mrs. Eneyo says, exasperated.

"Oh no," my father says, laughing, settling into a comfortable position. "No price. We'd just like a job so we can have enough money to get something like that boat of yours."

"This beauty?" Mr. Abalaka chuckles, patting his vessel tenderly. "We just like it because it runs on trash juice."

"Unfortunately," Mrs. Eneyo says, steering the conversation back to the point, "we don't really know of anything at the moment. Nothing's available. Sorry. But we could get you some fish. The good kind."

"That would be great," my father says. They exchange contact information. The three of them laugh and joke some more while Joseph and I sit quietly in the boat like the good children that we are, trying not to disturb them.

Eventually, they leave.

"That was fun," Joseph yawns, stretching his arms in the air.

My father nods, distracted. He taps our arms. "Better stretch those arms well, because we're following them."

"Why?" I groan, rubbing my lucky spoon, feeling around its edges.

"I want to see who they give all that trash to—see if we can get some of that hustle too," says my father.

"It's always nice to know that trust is the one thing you can look forward to in today's society," Joseph says, his voice dry, his expression deadpan, but Dad ignores him.

"Probably looking out for themselves, those two, and that's what we have to do too. Uncontaminated fish for garden eggs isn't a fair trade, and we don't even know if they're going to use that as some sort of leverage later on. The way I see it, we need to get jobs so we can have good money to negotiate with. *This* is how we do things."

"They could easily spot us," Joseph sighs, grabbing a paddle.

"That is why, today, we learn of other routes," my father says, chest out and proud. He looks happier than I've ever seen him, a pirate in open air.

This is the adventure I've been looking for, and I'm grateful that I'm here conspiring with my father, too tired to think about drowning.

To our surprise, we don't get caught. My father makes us wait until the man and woman are some distance ahead, and then we follow slowly. We watch as they haul trash and animals into their boat.

It's impressive.

We crack jokes and I laugh, forgetting my thoughts of death, feeling the wind in my hair, having a good time.

It's getting dark as Mr. Abalaka and Mrs. Eneyo stop in front of a large house on stilts, wooden and sturdy despite its rotting wood. It is painted a welcoming colour of blue and green, faded and moldy.

They get out of the boat and exchange their trash and game with a woman for stacks of money. My father's eyes widen when he sees it and he smiles like a hyena.

Mr. Abalaka and Mrs. Eyeno shake hands with the woman and get back into their boat.

We duck. Are they turning back, coming our way?

Luckily we don't have to deal with that stress because the two of them head further down the road in the opposite direction.

We wait thirty minutes in the dark. I doze and dream of legs that stop kicking, of going underwater . . . .

I wake up. My father and Joseph are asleep. I tap my father's shoulder and he jolts awake.

"Can we go and meet the woman they were talking to?" I ask.

"Sure, sure," says my father, still sleepy. "Paddle! Let's get this over with."

I wake Joseph up and we paddle slowly towards the house. My father gets out of the boat and knocks on the door.

Nobody answers.

Dad knocks again, harder.

An old woman storms out, her grey hair in curls, her dark skin covered in powder. She is wearing a long shirt and screaming at us in a heavy Yoruba dialect, each word thick and vicious like a curse.

"Ma," my father says, trying to placate her, but he backs away when she tries to slap him. "Please, we just came here looking for work. Any job, please, we'll do it."

The woman pauses for a second, thinks. "I only have two

workers. They're good, sturdy—"

"But not enough," says my father, smiling, trying to sell her on the idea of us.

"The problem is that they keep on getting rid of everyone I hire." She sighs, putting her hands to her chin. "You see, when I hire new people, the price goes down and their pay goes down, so . . . ."

"I understand," my father says, and sighs. "Sharing won't kill them."

"Okay, look," the woman says, yawning. "Whatever. They've proven themselves to be worthy of all I've given them, but I could be making a much bigger profit with more people. And my own employers will like having more of all these goods. So, I'll tell you what: I won't say anything about you guys to them. As long as you don't get discovered, you have the job."

"We won't accept the offer, but thanks anyway," Joseph spits, but Daddy only looks more decided.

"We accept," he says, and he and our new employer exchange numbers.

We row some way in silence. Joseph and Dad's faces are red and flushed.

"You know," my father starts, "our house is falling apart. We have a chance here. And we're doing so good here, that I think this could be our new life: downsized, out in the open air, near the sea—"

It's not a sea," Joseph corrects him, rowing faster. I can practically see the smoke rising from him, but I don't say anything. Nothing I do will distract him.

"Metaphorically," my father adds quietly.

"Leave me out of it," hisses Joseph, "because my part in this *adventure* is done."

Our mother is waiting for us at home. I've missed the classes she usually teaches me, maths and science and geometry, but I think Dad should get the crap for that. My arms ache.

Dad starts telling Mummy that she needs to increase her plant portions for her new customers, Mr. Abalaka and Mrs. Eyeno.

I follow Joseph to his room. He paces around, knocking into things. When he's stressed and angry, he cries. The tears don't stop running.

"If I could leave today, I would," he says. "The underwater program's not ready yet, so I guess we'll just have to wait and watch our father make a fool of himself every day."

I stay silent. My brother looks at me. Too closely, like he's searching my soul. And I flinch, because I don't want him discovering all the baggage inside me.

"Do you actually still want to go with Dad?"

"It's an adventure," I say quietly, trying to make myself believe it.

"B . . . but . . . what is wrong with you? He's out of control. Why are you even thinking like this?"

"This house is falling apart," I reply, my voice barely a whisper.

"We're going to leave," he yells. "We're hoping for a better future."

"Hope is never now," I mutter under my breath.

Maybe it's better to just float into oblivion, to row above the water till the moment I go under. Till the moment I'm nothing but fodder and infection, another rotting body in the stagnancy.

I can hear my father shouting at my mother in his room. I go out into the passage and he storms out, practically hyperventilating.

"What's going on?" I ask, and it feels like I'm the adult and he's the child.

"I don't want to talk about it."

I try again.

"Your mother doesn't want to join us in the canoes. And your brother thinks he's too good for us. But we, we are the ones who survive, who go the distance, who have adventures. Right?"

"Right," I say, my voice hollow.

"I'm going to sleep on the couch," he says. He goes downstairs.

I go into his room to find my mother. Her face is expressionless. "Is everything all right?" I say.

She gets out of bed. She drinks from the bottle of water at her bedside. "Do you know why I don't like to say anything to your father's ideas? He just . . . has this way of making people be the bad guy, the nag, and he sort of punishes us for it and enjoys doing so, being that person. And now that I'm silent, he hates it, because I'm refusing to engage, not playing my role. I was a little worried you were too much like him when you were growing up," she continues. "I was afraid I was going to have two of him in the house. I almost considered leaving. But you've made a personality for yourself and . . . I don't always understand you, Uti, but I think you'll be fine."

It's late and I go to bed, but I can't fall asleep in this house of broken relationships.

For a few days, I don't join my father when he goes out in the boat. I need to process things.

When I rejoin him, my father holds me close and brings out something from his hiking bag. I shriek when I see the gun.

"It's good," he tells me, but his eyes look fearful. "For protection. This one can take more bullets than you'd expect. And—" He flicks a button. "It has a silencer. A silent killer. This is for some cold-blooded killing."

"Hi there!" A voice calls out to us.

"Hide the gun," I say. An unpleasant chill runs down my spine.

I turn to see Mr. Abalaka and Mrs. Eyeno waving at us, a little distance away, a big bubble floating in their hands full of . . . fish. Corporate companies hand out free samples of these easily disposable bubbles for storing things. We row towards them, and I feel an unbearable tension in my heart, yet my father's happy expression forces me to plaster a thick, fake smile on my face.

We come up alongside them, and before they say anything, they pop the bubble and the fish falls into our boat. Fresh-looking, uncontaminated, pure fish.

"Oh, wow, that was fast," my father says, too quickly,

scratching his head, nervous. "We haven't got the eggs yet."

"Oh, hey, no, we're not pressuring you; take your time," Mr. Abalaka says. He laughs and waves a hand at us.

"As long as you bring it," Mrs. Eyeno adds.

We are silent.

"How's work?" My father asks.

I feel like shrivelling up into a ball.

"It's good," they say, simultaneously.

I force a chuckle, trying to look relaxed.

"We're actually hoping for a promotion for all the good work we've been doing," Mr. Abalaka says.

My father and I share a look.

"Yeah, you know, at the end of the month," Mrs. Eyeno says, sorting a piece of trash.

"Wow, that's fascinating," I say. "But I actually think it's time for us to go. Right, Daddy?"

"Absolutely. Yeah, thank you for the fish; good looking pieces of meat. We'll get those garden eggs to you soon."

We watch them row away, and we're finally able to breathe.

My father looks at me and nods in approval. "Listen, that was great. Especially as I just got a text from our employer asking us to catch a crocodile. We'll just have to stay out of their way till it's time for us to meet the boss tomorrow."

"Won't they also be dropping off their goods then?"

"Oh no. Our employer changed their drop-off date. She said they were suspicious, but she thinks it's fine because they won't find out."

I nod, putting all my effort into rowing the boat single-handed as we go around the markets looking for parasitic feed and hunting equipment. While my father prices and bargains, I rub my spoon. It feels like my last claim to innocence.

"Are you ready?" My father asks me, and I shrug.

We row towards the nearest gutters. I feel so different from who I was when we started doing this, now that we are throwing caution to the wind.

"So, you'll do the luring and I'll kill," my father tells me, handing me a pair of high-tech binoculars. I aim them at the shadows that swim in the water, trying to identify a crocodile.

I lower the baited trap into the water. I try to breathe and relax.

"Now," my father says, "we wai—"

The crocodile jumps aboard, snapping and angry, and almost submerges our boat. The wire trap pokes into its skin as it roars, its breath disgusting, its large teeth reaching for me. Large pieces of glass stab into the beast's head and broken cans stick out of its body like piercings. Nylon bags are draped over this creature that is trying to eat me, and I scream and scream. I feel like my heart has stopped. Memories of my hollow existence overwhelm me as I wait for the moment I have been dreading.

Death is coming.

My father shoots it in the head, his hand steady. The crocodile jerks, spurting blood, then lies still. Daddy looks rattled, terrified, and I am a bloody mess. "We did it," my father says.

Immediately when we get home, I storm into my brother's room, leaving my father to hide the crocodile's body in the garage, letting Joseph see me in all my wretchedness.

Joseph leaps up and reaches for me and wraps me in his arms. "Oh my God! What the hell happened?"

"He's out of control," I say. I can't stop crying. I'm a snotty mess.

"Now will you listen to me?" says Joseph.

"No," I say, pushing him away. "We need to help Dad. You, especially, have to be there to ground him and make sure this doesn't happen again. We need you. Come back."

He says nothing. I hear no objections. I believe it's agreement.

The next morning, I worry my brother won't show up as I wait downstairs. But Joseph does come, and I feel like I can do it knowing that he's with me.

He and Daddy look at each other, the silence between them distressing.

But my father gives a nod of approval and we set out relaxed.

My brother lays down the law and gets Dad to put the gun away, telling him we should just concentrate on the trash after all the trouble he caused yesterday. Joseph still doesn't look too happy, but at least my father stays silent.

Instead, Dad spends the time trying to call our employer, who isn't picking up. The boss communicates on her terms, not ours.

I tap my brother's shoulder just as he's about to dive into the water again, a rope around his waist. "Aren't you going to let me—"

"No," he says sternly. "You're not doing anything after what happened yesterday. Just secure the rope to the boat."

I attach the rope in silence and just wish for this day to be over.

Hours pass.

At last, the day ends. My brother and I row over to the house on stilts, our arms sore. We wait while my father knocks repeatedly. I notice a boat sticking out slightly at the back of the house. I rub my eyes.

Mr. Abalaka and Mrs. Eyeno open the door. Their clothes are covered in blood, their hands hidden.

We freeze.

We stare until if feels as if the silence is going to kill us.

"What-t-t are you doing here?" My father stutters, doing his best to smile.

"We thought we'd rest in our new home and wait for the people who caused our schedule to change," Mrs. Eyeno spits, then smiles.

"We got that promotion we were talking about," Mr. Abalaka says.

My father nods, looking petrified. Joseph slowly reaches for the paddle.

"You know," my father says, his voice too desperate as he reaches for the gun bag, "this is all a big misunderstanding."

"Right," they say.

They're quick. Mrs. Eyeno has a pistol. A bullet to the head and Joseph collapses into the water. I scream as my father grabs his gun. Mr. Abalaka's spear stabs into his gut before he can fire. He follows Joseph into the water.

Into the water, into the water; everything dead and into the water. Water red with blood.

I scramble and I scream. I piss my pants. I think, *death comes*, as they approach the boat. I'm so full of grief and anger and terror.

They are going to kill me. Am I prepared?

To our legs, to our bones, to our muscles, to our eyes ....

I reach into my pocket. I pull back my arm and stab the spoon into Mr. Abalaka's eye.

He screams and drops his spear. Mrs Eyeno tries to stop the blood.

I jump into the water and start swimming away. I swim so hard in all the mutation and infection, all the things that have tried to drown me, all the things that have tried to kill me.

I can't breathe right. I can't live right. My brother and father, gone into the water.

But I can't drown. I can't fall, I can't stop myself escaping.

Because I need to get back to my community, I need to tell my mother about Joseph's dreams of underwater living, about his hopeful future that better come quickly because I'm done waiting.

I'm alone in this vast, polluted space, but I know which direction to go in. I'll find my way home.

Osahon Ize-Iyamu writes speculative fiction. He is a graduate of the Alpha Writers Workshop and his work has been published in *Clarkesworld*, *The Dark*, and *Sword and Sonnet*. You can find him online @osahon4545

Flowers for the Living, Flowers for the Dead

Michelle Muenzler

Strange how even in the dark, the eyes find shape.

"The walls are made of flowers," Amelie says, nestled against me. "White flowers, bigger than I can hold."

"White as clouds," I say. "Bright and soft." Our voices are muted. Collapsed into the space we occupy, just as the space has collapsed into us.

"They smell . . . they smell like butter."

I try to remember the smell of flowers. Of petals. Of wind. "Yes," I say, finally giving up. "Like butter. Like butter and rain."

A minute passes. An hour. A month. A day. Time has little meaning in the land of the dead.

Amelie shifts beside me. But not too much. There's so little space, so much of it filled.

"Mama, I feel rain. It must be pouring outside."

There is no outside. Not anymore. "Yes, pouring like a molten kettle."

"It's hot. So hot it sizzles when it strikes the mud."

"So hot when it strikes, the mud turns to stone."

"So hot," she says, whispering, "it makes the world turn."

I pause. "So hot, it makes the world burn."

More silence. Hours. Seconds. Millennia.

"The flowers are gone," Amelie says. Somber now. "They've burned with everything else, haven't they?"

I find her hand in the darkness. Squeeze. "It's okay, baby. We'll just plant more."

The world outside is burning. But here in the land of the dead nothing burns.

"I'm hungry," Amelie says.

My abdomen is a creaking hollow. My chest, my skull. "The dead can't be hungry, baby."

Shapes flicker in the darkness. Rabbits. Dogs. The flamingo I saw once when I was nine.

"But I *am* hungry," Amelie says.

"Shh." I pull her against me.

She's cold—but I suppose you can't be dead and not be cold as well. Still. I didn't expect her to be this cold.

"Here," I say, setting my hand in hers, "have some bread."

Even dead, it's hard not to feel when she begins to chew.

In the dark, the shapes are always changing. They are also always the same.

"Do you think it's over?" Amelie asks. "Do you think it's safe again?"

How long has it been? Time dances in the land of the dead, like angels on the head of a pin. But however long it's been, it will never be enough. The world can't burn forever, but it can burn longer than us.

"Come here," I say, and take Amelie into my arms. I curl around her in the dark, like the shell of an egg. I should hurt, but here in the land of the dead there is no pain. Or hunger.

Or sorrow.

Amelie's hand grazes my cheek. "It's raining again," she says. Wipes a droplet free.

"Yes," I say, and squeeze her tight. Like I'll never let her go. "It's always raining here, in the land of the dead."

And on the walls, again, the flowers grow.

Michelle Muenzler, known at local science fiction and fantasy conventions as "The Cookie Lady", writes fiction both dark and strange to counterbalance the sweetness of her baking. Her short fiction and poetry can be read in numerous science fiction and fantasy magazines, and she takes immense joy in crinkling words like little foil puppets. Find links to her work at michellemuenzler.com, and if you are feeling especially brave, check out her squidgy weird novella, "The Hills of Meat, the Forest of Bone", on Amazon.

She promises it won't bite. Much.

The Mortmain

Sebastian Strange

Henryk Król was washing dishes, looking out at the setting-sun light shuddering through the trees—considering, without real conviction, whether the trees should be trimmed to let more light through; whether he had any right to trim the trees, as after years of residence he was still unsure where his yard ended and the forest began—when the boy knocked on the edge of his screen door and came into the kitchen a moment later. Henryk had fallen out of the habit of locking his door during the day; here, it was unnecessary. And locking your door at night was only because of the animals, raccoons with their thieving ways and curious deer, occasionally a bear. Not boys with bare feet.

"What happened to your shoes?" Henryk asked. Even little boys did not run around barefoot like they used to. And this boy existed in the grey area between boy and man, slight enough to be a teenager, wiry and solemn enough to be a young man. He wore ripped trousers and a grey hoodie worn so thin in patches Henryk could glimpse his ribs; no shirt, no shoes. The boy seemed unreal, like a preview of his usual unsettling dreams.

"Nothing," the boy said. "Are you the surgeon?"

Henryk dried his hands, keeping the boy in the corner of his eye. "I was a surgeon. Why do you ask?"

The boy tugged his hoodie off, scattering pine needles across the floor. The scent of the forest moved into the kitchen. Using his skinny hands to frame the area, he indicated a patch of skin on his stomach that looked exactly the same as the rest. "There's something hurting me," he said flatly. "It needs to be taken out."

Henryk moved slowly as he picked the hoodie up and handed it back to the boy, who took it reluctantly. He felt like he was in a room with a wild animal. Didn't want to spook it. "What is your name?"

The boy glanced over his shoulder. "Mort."

A blatant falsehood: the forest behind him was the Mortmain Forest. Henryk let it slide. "Mort, I am several years retired. Also, you must be examined before you have surgery. Have you been examined?"

Mort scowled. "I don't need it. I know what's wrong."

"How?"

"I feel it." He touched the place again, gently. "I know when something's wrong. I just can't fix it." He looked at Henryk imperiously. "Aren't you supposed to help people?"

"I am supposed to help my patients. There is a process to becoming a patient. I would not want to hurt anyone by rushing into something."

Mort's scowl deepened. "Didn't you take an oath?"

"The Hippocratic? That would have been foolish of me. It prohibits the use of a knife, among other outdated stipulations."

"*I solemnly pledge to consecrate my life to the service of humanity.* That one."

Henryk looked at Mort with new interest. "The Declaration of Geneva. It's less well-known."

Mort didn't provide an explanation, just gestured at his stomach, get-to-it-then. Henryk sighed. "It still does not mean I must tend anyone who comes to me. You may need help, but unless you are examined I cannot tell whether you need the help of a surgeon or . . . another sort of doctor."

With an angry huff of breath, Mort pulled the hoodie back on. "I don't need another doctor. I need your help."

"You don't know—"

"I know what I need." Mort turned and went out, looking back as the screen door shivered in its frame. "I'll be back," he said. "You'll change your mind."

"Unless you come back with paperwork from a doctor, I shall not."

"You have to," Mort said. The hoarseness of his voice made it either a threat or a statement of desperation. He turned, then, and half-ran into the trees. Henryk watched until night swelled up—as it seemed to in these parts, rising up from the ground like mist—and made every tree a shadow in the dark.

Henryk often questioned why he lived by the Mortmain. The trees were lovely, if old and tangled, but he preferred cities. The convenience, the bustle of life, never being quite alone. His husband—Simon—had liked the forest. Bought this house. Maybe some lingering superstition had drawn Henryk out here; his mother always said ghosts haunted the places they loved the most.

No ghosts out here, unless Mort was one. Seeking eternal help for a hernia that had killed him in the days before medicine advanced. He looked nothing like Simon—Simon had been taller, dark-skinned and vibrant. No better word to describe how alive he felt to Henryk, right up until he wasn't.

Late afternoon, a day later, Henryk walked to the nearby town. He argued with himself, like always, over how whether he should get a car. He had learned to drive once, and he chose to believe that, like riding a bicycle, it was muscle memory. But the process of buying one, the noise and intensity and all the myriad little things that had been added to cars since he had last owned one—it daunted him. Better to walk, until he could no longer.

He asked the young woman at the grocery store if she knew anyone who looked like Mort. She shook her head. "Could be a couple different boys from around here. Probably someone messing around, trying to scare you."

"Then they did not succeed."

She laughed. Henryk was reminded, uncomfortably, that he had become what certain young women see as *a cute old man*. Soft-voiced and nonthreatening and slow, with a funny accent.

Do you know what I did when I was your age? He wanted to say. *I crossed an ocean, moved to a different country—this unfriendly country—to be with the man I loved. I never thought I would grow old, but I have. Alone. It's not amusing.*

He smiled, with effort, instead. Time would talk to the girl in his stead, say things more eloquently than he ever could.

"Hey," she said, sliding him his bags, "you need any help with those?"

"I will be fine."

"The development's not happening on your side of the forest, is it? Things are getting pretty hairy around there."

"This is the first I have heard of it."

She leaned her elbows on the counter and pointed out the window. "If you go up to the corner of Pine and Elm, you can see the smoke and dust. The government cut a deal with some company that wants to take a slice off the Mortmain and put something in—probably a luxury hotel or something stupid like that."

"That's terrible."

The girl nodded. "And that's not even the weird part. The weird part is, something's been coming out of the woods at night and messing with the machines. Overturning them, scratching them up—*huge* machines! One guy tried to get a look at it—I dunno what problem they had with their cameras—and now he's in the hospital."

"Perhaps a bear?"

"It'd have to be a hell of a bear. My aunt says it's karma. She was protesting down there before they shooed everyone off because of the whatever-it-is." The girl sighed. "They're probably gonna get a permit to shoot it, because God forbid the wildlife trespass on the bit of the forest they want to wreck."

Henryk looked her over again, taking in her carved-wood earrings, the environmental pin on her apron. "You would prefer the creature chase them away, I imagine."

"Who wouldn't?" She shook her head. "But it seems like every forest's being torn apart these days. If it isn't us, it's beetles, rot . . . ."

"Always something."

She rubbed the pin with a tip of her finger, as if it were a magic charm. "That's life, I guess."

Mort was sitting on the steps when Henryk came up to the house, a still, dark figure in the twilight. He wore shoes this time—sneakers, the logo long peeled away, splitting at one seam—without socks, and the same grey hoodie and trousers.

"I can't give you what you want," Henryk said.

Without answering, Mort came forward and took a grocery bag. Henryk yielded it with only slight reluctance; his arms ached. Mort hefted it like a dead leaf. When he opened the door—which Henryk could not recall if he'd locked—and went into the kitchen, he didn't bother to turn on the lights. He moved in the dark like he knew the place.

They put things away together, silently. Mort still smelled like pine and oak, but with a sour whiff of oil and smoke. His hands were striped with dirt. When they finished, Henryk pointed down the hall. "The bathroom is down there. You may use the shower if you wish."

He watched Mort leave the room, wondering if he lived in the forest. Judging by the degraded state of his clothes, maybe he was a runaway; Henryk could, with some work, imagine a teenager being too stubborn to return to civilization even if they needed clothes or medical help. Perhaps he had fled an abusive home. Or maybe that was the wrong train of thought; maybe he had come to the Mortmain to join the protesters and chosen to go into the woods he loved instead of going back home when they were dispersed.

He made tea.

"It's only going to get worse," Mort said from the doorway.

Henryk had seen a lot of things in his life; he only blinked before saying, "I believe you forgot your clothes."

Mort rolled his eyes, as if Henryk was changing the subject for foolish reasons, and wandered back down the hall. He left a pattern of water on the floor behind him, footprints that didn't look quite right. When he returned he wore only his pants and shoes; his hoodie, ripped down a seam, was draped over his arm. On the lower left side of his stomach, there was a small dark spot.

"What is that?"

Mort glared at him. "The same thing it was yesterday."

"The skin was unmarked yesterday." Henryk beckoned him closer and examined the spot. Discolored skin, no break. "This may simply be a bruise. They sometimes look unusual."

Mort sighed. "It's underneath. It's just starting to show now."

"Mort," Henryk said, keeping his tone casual, "do you have a family?"

"Yes. I haven't seen my parents in a long time, but my younger brother lives with me."

"Are you old enough to be living alone?"

"I'm plenty old."

"You ripped your hoodie. Do you have anything else?"

Mort shrugged.

He was taller and a little thinner than Henryk, but one of Henryk's old shirts fit him well enough. Henryk expected him to protest, but he accepted it—and the trousers Henryk offered—with a confused air. Like he couldn't understand why Henryk would turn down his request and then give him something he hadn't asked for. "Won't you just trust me and take it out?" he asked one more time.

Henryk said, "Go to the doctor down in the town—do you need his address?"

Mort shook his head. "That's too far," he said, and wouldn't explain what he meant.

Henryk dreamed strange dreams that night; different from his usual stressed, repetitive dreams about strangers telling him Simon had died; or his whole life unwinding like a spool of thread until he was back in his childhood home, where nobody knew him. Simon came and sat on his bed, looking younger. He thanked Henryk for burying him in the woods—which was wrong; Henryk had seen him buried under a tree in the city cemetery. He tried to say this, but his tongue was dark and swollen, and when he pressed a hand to his ribs, his flesh gave way like overripe fruit. Simon frowned, the same sweet, concerned look Henryk had seen so many times, and said, "Honey, I think you're sick." He smelled oil and smoke.

When he woke, sweaty and short of breath, his stomach ached. He went out to sit on his steps, although it was pitch-black. The night air was sweet and cool; his shivering abated after a few minutes. Far away, he heard a machine start up and then die again. Start up, and die. The third time it choked and sputtered to a stop like an animal with its throat opened, and after that there were only the small noises of the woods.

Online, Henryk only found an article or two about the permission given to pass a road through and build something on "the edge" of the Mortmain; after some time he finally found an informal news outlet covering the protesters and "the large animal" that had disturbed the proceedings. That article questioned the government's authority to give permission for the land to be used; the true ownership of the Mortmain seemed murky.

He had to go into town to hear that one of the machines had been flipped over and split like a cracked nut the night before. The people in charge had chased onlookers away but it only took one or two for the whole town to know. The man in the hospital had woken up and told a nurse that a "monster" had thrown him into a tree. On the local news station, a spokesperson for the project assured everyone it was probably a bear. "Clearly aggressive," he said. "Probably sick with something. But there's no need to worry, we'll get it sorted out."

At some point during the day, the feeling of Simon's presence settled in behind him like a shadow. Henryk did his best to ignore it, then did his best to confront it. His mirror showed him nothing but himself, on the tired side of sixty-five but alive, relatively healthy. Not dying, not rotting, not haunted. He focused on the silent air behind his shoulder, tried to picture Simon there.

"Why now?" he asked.

There was nothing but silence and an answer from his own memories. Simon coming home waxy with hunger and weariness, red-eyed from smoke, bruised and battered. Simon going out again; *every person counts, Henryk, we have to make our voices heard. Have to show them they can't get away with this.* There had always been another march he wanted to join, another group he wanted to support, another injustice to protest. Right up until he couldn't.

"But there is nothing I can do," Henryk told the mirror.

This time, the silence sounded like Mort.

That night, Mort did not come.

The next day, Mort did not come.

The third day, in the morning, Henryk was washing his coffee cup when a tree crashed somewhere outside, and shots rang out. He dropped the cup, it shattered into pieces in the blood-warm water, and he moved outside like a sleepwalker.

Somehow he expected to step into the past. Into a memory he did not have, because he had not been there the day Simon and his friends had been stopped by the police. He hadn't witnessed the questions, if there had been any, or the word or motion that had made one man pull his trigger—the "accidental" shot that had clipped one of Simon's more important arteries.

The past did not wait outside, nor even down the path. Instead, he smelled smoke and blood, and just beyond the first bend towards the town, saw a few men standing around a great humped form bigger than a bear. Bigger than two. The men were murmuring to each other, white-faced. The gunshots he had heard were only the latest; small dark holes spilling rusty trails of blood covered the beast's side and head. As he drew closer, still moving as if hypnotized, he saw that the creature had brown fur and clawed feet, but its lolling head was like that of a malformed deer. Three eyes glistened up at the sky, sightless and beginning to cloud over.

He wondered if it had a small dark spot on its lower left stomach.

And before the men could look up and see him, he ran.

Back at his house, the shock and exertion struck him like a brick to the stomach. He leant against the door, holding his side, holding himself together, and wheezed with humorless laughter. Simon had always teased him about being a surgeon who did not look after his own body. Told him he'd regret it when he was old. Henryk had always agreed, but he had never got around to eating the right things or taking up jogging. Sleeping regular hours had never been anything but a pipe dream.

He thought maybe he should move back to the city, take a fitness class so he could better run away from dead monsters and the fools that shot them. With every ragged breath, he lost a bit of hope that this could be a dream. The dead . . . thing, whatever it was, *whoever* it was, remained seared into his mind.

On the news, later, they said they'd shot a large bear.

That night, Henryk heard breathing outside, almost lost in the wind; heavy, thick breathing like an animal in pain. Unsettled, he ventured out onto the porch. Something moved by the trees: to his unadjusted eyes, a formless shadow.

The breathing went low, gulping. The way you cry after you have cried for hours, when you'd stop if you knew how, because your eyes are sore and your throat gluey. Henryk blinked a few times, made out the shape of the shadow. "Mort?"

He barely expected an answer—part of him was sure Mort had been shot that morning—but the shadow raised its head. A moment later he made out Mort's reddened eyes, the downwards slash of his mouth. He took a deep breath, then winced, and Henryk's eyes went down to where Mort's hand was firmly clamped over his left side. Something wet seeped through the fabric of his shirt, and an oily, rotten-fruit odour filled the air.

"Today," Mort said, "they killed my younger brother."

Henryk took a step forward. "Come inside."

Mort made as if to move forward, then flinched back, catching at a branch to steady himself. "Can't." His voice was a croak.

"Mort," Henryk said, desperate, "I don't understand any of this. I can't help you if I don't understand."

Mort was already turning, shuffling back into the woods. "Don't have . . . to understand," he said, almost inaudible. "Just . . . ."

Henryk wondered how he had ever thought Mort was young;

he could recognize how another old man moved even in the dark at the edge of the forest. He stood gripping the railing until his knuckles began to ache, while the forest murmured and moaned and foreboding built within him like in one of his old dreams. When he moved, he went to find a knife.

He stood in the kitchen, staring at his knife block with the beginnings of despair. A thought struck him. A minute's search and he'd located the scalpel he'd used as a letter opener, back when he got mail that wasn't financial. The blade was dull, but it would have to do. The wind was picking up outside and there was a stink in it, apparent even through the windows.

Wrapping a scarf over his nose and mouth, he walked out into the woods.

He did not move into the trees so much as the trees seemed to leap forward and surround him, bending their heavy heads together, muttering at him in languages he couldn't understand. Six yards into the forest he found Mort's sneakers, decayed. Two yards more and Henryk glimpsed the shirt he'd lent Mort, now wet and torn, pierced by the limb of a tree. Mold-white liquid spattered the leaves underneath it, and the slow drip of it stayed with him until he could no longer see the world outside the forest.

A few yards ahead, a shadow rose up. "Hurry," it said. For a moment, moonlight slid over the face of a woman: a face he'd seen on Missing posters in town five years gone. Her voice dry wood creaking, beetles gnawing. Her eyes wet and round, black, like a deer's. "You have to go further in."

"Which way?"

A half-decayed arm rose, then the body fell like a card castle. Henryk moved on, skirting the corpse. He wondered how many had gone missing in these woods, when the boy that the Mortmain had possessed had died here, and for a moment a hysterical laugh pressed at the back of his throat. It seemed impossible that something was killing this hungry, killing creature. That it was asking for help.

The wind cut through the heavy branches, making them groan, and stray raindrops pattered down. The clouds above looked heavy and wrong; he thought of acid rain, and quickened his pace. Further in; that was always the way, wasn't it? There must be, somewhere, people who kept things neat and separate. Went to work and volunteered a handful of hours a week and got drunk with their friends, the mythic work-life balance. Simon and Henryk, though, had gotten along because they were all or nothing. Nothing Henryk wouldn't do for Simon except give up surgery, the hard hours and the harder work. Nothing, vice versa, except Simon had his causes—all of them, because—well, he'd always joked it was because God had given him a heaping armful of it to deal with. Couldn't just be black. Couldn't just be queer. Couldn't just be a tree-hugger. *I'm just living,* he'd say. *Just trying to live with what I am and what I need. A job and love and air to breathe.*

He had none of those now, and Henryk only had air; some days he felt as dead above the earth as Simon was dead beneath it. Not tonight. Tonight the air was electric and raw and rank with illness: the illness in Mort's belly, and in the woods, and echoing, hollow and rotten, in Henryk's own body. He might be dying, but he wasn't dead yet.

The same could be said for Mort.

Henryk found him after he'd walked long enough to wonder if he'd come out the other side of the woods. He came out in a clearing instead, where Mort lay curled on the ground. He shucked his coat and unwound his scarf, despite the smell, and knelt down at Mort's side. Out of the corner of his eye, he saw animals among the trees: silent grey squirrels and dark birds he couldn't name. A few deer, too, and a great hulk that might have been a bear. It felt like an old operating theater, with an audience following his every movement.

"Said it would get worse," Mort said, his breathing labored. Henryk would have deserved it if the sentence was angry, smug, but it wasn't; it was simply resigned.

Henryk almost said, *I'm sorry,* but that would do nothing. "I'm here," he said gently. "I'm here now. You need to move your hands."

Mort's hands were clamped, bloodless, over the purpled skin of his stomach. There was an unpleasant sheen of wetness, as if something was sweating out through the injured skin. The skin itself looked bruised from the inside. Henryk thought about wasps that laid their young in other creatures, alien implanted things that ate their hosts, and his stomach turned over. He swallowed, didn't let it show. "Please," he said. "I'll help you."

Mort breathed hard, his eyes finally moving to fix on Henryk. He was not young, but for a moment his power and arrogance gleamed through, showed like a challenge in his eyes, and Henryk knew why he'd seemed young.

Henryk took out his scalpel, and Mort drew his stiff fingers away from the infected center of the wound.

The skin was so thin and degraded it parted like wet paper under the scalpel's edge, curling away from the seeping dark. Something moved deep within the opening, burying itself under flesh—earth?—and Henryk knew what he needed to do. Mort's wide, white-ringed eyes were fixed on him, desperate, the challenge gone out like a flame. Henryk smiled at him, gently.

"It will be all right," he said. "Close your eyes."

The animals around them stirred restlessly, but Mort nodded and did as he was told.

Henryk plunged his hand into the opening.

His vision split: in one thin, half-transparent panel of reality he pushed his hand into the dry stomach cavity of a corpse, crouching in an empty clearing as the rain started coming down. In another he dug into the wet, dark earth and the trees thrashed around him as if they were in pain. In another he parted the hairy skin of a monster shivering and trying to keep its limbs still against the ground, and reached in among its organs. In another he knelt over the whole town, trying not to crush the buildings with his knees as he pressed his fingertips into the edge of the forest, and a man ran over one of his fingers, his feet tickling like an ant's legs. In another, in another, in another—in half a dozen of his shattered visions Simon stood behind him among the trees. He was dead, he was not, there was blood on his pristine brown shirt, he smiled without smiling. But all of him stepped forward to put his hands on Henryk's shoulders.

"You got this, honey," he said, with one voice.

Henryk closed his eyes, shutting out all he saw, and focused on what was under his hand. Earth and flesh mingled, coexisting somehow—and a furtive, ugly movement underneath a lip of organ. Prying the opening wider, he reached in with his other hand and lifted a bit of Mort's intestine. The thing hidden under it tried to retreat, but he caught it in his free hand; it stung, struggling against his palm. His hand began to go numb.

"Well done," Simon said, so quiet Henryk could have

imagined it.

When he opened his eyes, Simon was gone. He knelt in a small, natural clearing as the rain began to fall, and only one grey squirrel remained of the animal audience. The white tail of a departing deer whisked away into the darkness. His scalpel was rusted in his hand, as if it had lain out in the woods for years. There was a sunken place in the ground in front of him, almost six feet long.

"Mort?" he asked. There was no reply. But he felt something jerk hard in his right hand, though it was numb and purpled with bruises and clenched so tight he could barely open it. When he did, something greyish and small dropped to the ground and began to trundle away like a beetle.

He stepped on it. Smoke rose from the crushed remains, but the rain put out the tiny smoldering, and the foul smell faded from the air.

Henryk walked home, slow with pain, through the scents of petrichor and lightning, and when he got there he sat on the front steps listening to the woods. Through the rain he couldn't see the thick smoke and the dust coming off the worksite—the place the worksite had been, because somehow he knew it had become a raw crater, a deep wound, but clean, ready to heal. The poison had been drawn out. His hand was numb. He thought, with tired amusement, of going to the doctor he'd urged Mort to visit in town. In the morning, though.

For now, he breathed the wet, clean air and *felt* the smoke, out in the distance, and the many-eyed creature that moved unsteadily through the forest, its belly healing, the human skin it had worn cast aside. Somewhere out in the woods, their dearest ones were buried side by side; somewhere out in the woods, the beetles ate and axes fell. But here, the Mortmain crooned to itself, like a cat purring or a child singing to soothe themselves when there was nobody to hold them after a hard surgery, and Henryk closed his eyes, pressed his good hand over his stomach and felt the rain washing away the sickness, unsure where he ended and the forest began.

Sebastian Strange grew up in New England and still feels like a New Englander, despite living in Ohio. His stories have appeared in *Mythic Delirium* and *Glittership*.

Extinction Dish

Carrie Reichardt

Carrie Reichardt is a self-titled 'craftivist'. Her work blurs the boundaries between craft and activism, using the techniques of muralism, mosaic and screen-printing to create intricate, highly-politicised works of art.

Song of the Suburbs

Christine Holland Cummings

Our houses are decaying   plants wait to take control   no they
    don't wait   they ceaseless
send their rootlings along the soil's pathways   wheedling   their
    limbs unwind   across
blank   space   filling up with light   blocking
    the light

Meanwhile in the East   snow presses its heavy breast   against
    the eaves of a ranch house
the gutters tear away   sheets of packed ice lance   to the ground
    watch out!

Our neighborhoods erode   woodpeckers drill utility poles
    kerkerkerkerkerkerkerkerkerker   how do they move their heads
so fast we wonder   but they do   holes accumulate
    a lacework   someday they'll topple   and then
kablammo   no more power

Oak roots down below   thrust up   concrete sidewalks
    bust up   Maintenance!   Maintenance!
someone call the city   the sidewalk's all ajumble

And the freeways oh the freeways are a mess
    just look at all the new holes   every time it rains
        the veritable earth   dropping   out   pulling   away
    the asphalt   withdrawing
      Never mind never mind   we'll shelter in our houses
    until we can no more

Kestrel in an Apocalyptic Landscape

Christine Holland Cummings

Kestrel: (from French crécerelle, derivative from crécelle, i.e. ratchet)

Also known as windhover because he can hover, even in still air, but when he
hovers he usually faces toward a breeze, no matter how slight.

Gerard Manley Hopkins wrote

Dapple-dawn-drawn Falcon, in his riding / of the rolling level underneath him steady air . . . .

Say that aloud: in his riding / of the rolling level underneath him steady air . . . .

rolling level underneath him steady   five troches that roll along
like a wave, cresting and falling, cresting and falling   and land lightly   on air

In some future time and place a kestrel perches on a leafless branch on a leafless tree, waits
for something to stir. The landscape is open, naked, brown as his dominant plumage (but oh
the blue-gray of his wings, the black streak descending from his eye like a tear).

With a push he sends himself into the rolling level underneath him steady air. All is silent
except for the clack of his feathers as he holds himself upright facing into a breeze,
tailfeathers spread, wingfeathers spread, head bent like a penitent to scan the ground.

Scorpion.

He tilts and sleekens and spills himself down, talons thrusting, strikes.

Dead insect in claw he lifts and flaps back to his tree, to the hollow
space in its trunk, where
she waits for him with the new one, first to emerge from the clutch,
and only.

He drops his gift and she shares it with the hatchling.

Christine Holland Cummings lives in Menlo Park, California with her husband and dog, where she has turned her small suburban plot into a native plant wildlife habitat. Her poems have appeared in *Bellowing Ark, Blueline, Hamilton Stone Review, Manzanita Quarterly, The Sand Hill Review, Blue Arc, Dark Matter: Women Witnessing*, an anthology of California poets from Tebot Bach Press, and a poetry anthology about loss of companion animals titled *Our Last Walk.*

Fuck You Pay Me

Francis Bass

In Indonesia the IAP was shelling Jakarta, in China the PLA Navy was scouring the Eastern seaboard for survivors, in the UK Londoners were lining up at WFP stations for groceries, and, just twenty miles from Felix and Anya, in Muscatine the combined forces of the Louisa, Muscatine, Scott, and Cedar County police departments were performing rescue missions and responding to bouts of looting throughout the flooded riverfront of the city—but in Greatland, Iowa, it was a quiet first day of winter break.

Felix and Anya sat on the bench swing at Washington Park, a treeless half-block of muddy grass with a small playground complex, not far from their high school. They were holding each other's cold-numbed hands, Felix stamping against the ground occasionally to swing the bench.

"I found a personal accountancy AI calibrated for the Midwest," Anya said, "if you want to check that out?"

"I thought you said personal accountancy was impossible to calculate."

"I don't think I said that," Anya murmured.

"Yes you did, because I was asking you about these credit tallies people use when they go looting." Felix turned F's gaze on Anya.

"Oh. Um. I think I didn't say that. But I might've said it's . . . well, it would be *nearly* impossible to make one that was global, but regional ones are easier. There's one for England, I know, people have used it to make credit tallies."

"Sure, let's do it then. I bet your credit's a lot higher than mine. My parents and parents' parents and parensparensparens are European as shit."

Anya pulled her hand away to take out her cellphone, an old utilitarian thing that she had never gotten an upgrade for as long as Felix had known her. "Okay, here," she said, handing F her phone. The website had just a few text fields on it—place of residence, ethnicity, and class—but as Felix answered them, they branched out into further questions of religion, great grandparents' nationality, gender, assigned gender, time of immigration, and many fields where F had to write "IDK" and move on. When F tapped the "Submit" button, the phone looked like it was crashing, but then a results screen came up. "Nine hundred and forty-eight dollars!" Felix yelled. "Holy shit! If that's what I'm owed, I can't imagine what your credit is!"

"Yeah, neat huh?" Anya said, taking her phone back. "I'm thinking of pulling some old census data to a make a mod that can handle inputs about Iowa counties—get more specific on it, you know?"

As she started to tuck the phone into her pocket, Felix cut in, "Wait, you're not going to see what *you're* owed? Come on, you've got to—I bet it's a shitload."

"I mean, but. I know that. I kind of already know. N'COBRA developed an AI to calculate reparations, and you can just split that number by the number of people in the US descended from slaves."

"But this is for you—you *personally*. Come on, for me, I want to know."

"Okay," she took out her phone again, and smirked.

"What? What's funny?"

"It does kind of seem fun."

"It is fun!" Felix gave them a good swing, and stared out at the slushy ground while Anya entered her info. A truck, a gas guzzler, rumbled past them, and Felix shouted, "Fuck you!"

"Felix," Anya cautioned.

"Who the hell is still driving cars—and a gas car especially. Must be some POFA asshole, if they can afford to fuel that thing."

"Okay, just . . . ." Anya started, but then stopped and pursed her lips.

"What, what is it?"

That smirk broke out again, and she turned the phone screen to Felix: $104,667.

"Holy shit! That's enough for . . . that's enough for . . . ."

"A full ride to Iowa State," Anya said.

"What?" Felix asked. "But you've—"

"I've got the Future Scientists scholarships. Yeah, yeah. I just mean, if that money got frozen, or something, like they did with the scholarships for everyone who's a junior now . . . just a possibility, you know?"

Of course F knew. They both knew. And they both knew that Felix's legacy scholarship wasn't state-funded, so no one was going to pull *that* money to deal with the recession, and they both knew that if Future Scientists got cancelled, Felix would still be at Iowa State next year, while Anya—

"Yeah." Felix nodded and tried to not think about it, putting F's arm around Anya. F gave them a push, and the chains of the swing squawked as they rocked gently.

"Hey, Felix—"

"What if we looted something," Felix said.

"What?"

"Between the two of us we have more than enough credit to justify it."

"Real funny."

"I've been reading articles about it, it's really pretty easy in places like this. Plenty of big empty mansions out in the country, rich owners gone away for winter break . . . ."

"You're not being serious, um, right?"

"Well it's a fun idea, isn't—" Felix stopped when F heard a rumbling behind them and turned. It was that same fairly new, dark blue Ford that had gone by earlier. "The fuck are they doing? Just cruising around for the fun of it?" Felix bent down to scoop up some mud.

"F," Anya said, "F, hey . . . ."

The car turned left, passing right in front of them, and Felix jumped up and hurled the mudball as hard as F could. It hit the back windshield with a *whap* like a thunder crack, reverberating in the empty block. Felix shouted, "You piece of—" but F's breath caught when the back lights flared red and the truck shrieked to a halt. "Shit!" F pivoted back to Anya and shouted, "Run!" Anya dashed for her bike, and Felix for F's, not looking behind. Without meaning to they both pushed off in opposite directions, but F couldn't turn back now. The streets were deserted, grimy with salt, mud, and puddled potholes, so F blasted through four-way stops, turning left and right and right and left, trying to lose F's self in the waffle-iron residential blocks of the town.

A thin drizzle was passing over Greatland just a few days before Christmas when Felix texted Anya, *Hey you should come over. Parents are out trying to sell the car.* Felix set F's phone aside on the couch and turned back to the YT News special F was watching. It was about the origins of the accounting AIs, how they'd been an open source reference tool for the UN climate change program before becoming the core of a global political movement. After a while, Felix paused the video and picked up F's phone again—no response. F started to text her, but as soon as F did, there was a little knock at the front door.

Felix answered the door to find Anya outside, her bike chained to the railing of the little staircase leading up to the prefab.

"Hey," she said. She looked beautiful, flushed from the ride over, a warm little glow of light against the suburban wasteland and sky of shadows.

"Hey," Felix said, and hugged her. "Come in!" F stepped back, then closed the door behind her. "So, I was—"

"Actually, Felix . . . I kind of, need to—I should've told you right away the other day, but it's hard, and I just . . . ." Anya paused for a while, and bit at her lip. "The state legislature voted last week to—they're pulling funds for Future Scientists. All funds. And my parents—well we don't know what's—"

"So you, you can't go to Iowa?" Felix asked.

Anya shifted her feet around. "The law could be reversed, but . . . but . . . ."

Felix felt tears boiling up around F's eyes. "That's bullshit! For years, people like that have been fucking over people like you, and now that the consequences of greed have caught up with them, they're still just taking care of their own first!"

Anya hesitantly held out her arms, "Um," then she stepped forward and hugged F. She was a little taller than Felix, and F pushed F's face into the crumply synthetic material of her winter coat. Going off to college without Anya. Freshman sophomore junior senior year without Anya. And Anya, brilliant Anya, smarter than anyone F knew Anya, consigned to some community college. "It's so unfucking fucking fucking fair!" Felix slurred into her shoulder.

"I know," she murmured. "I'm. I'm really grateful for everything I have, but—I *really* wanted to go to a university." She shivered against Felix and hugged F tighter. F hugged her tighter back. "I—" she started, then choked and fell silent.

The world was stupid and mean and—

"Oh!" Felix pushed back from her. "I forgot, what I wanted to talk to you about!" F sniffed, and grinned. "I found a place we can loot!"

"What? Felix . . . ." Anya rubbed at her eyes.

"All the more reason to loot it now, right?" Sniff.

"But . . . no, there's no way . . . looting that much money, that would be traced, or, or, if we stole stuff and pawned it, it'd be really suspicious, and—"

"There are safe ways to do it though—online, you—"

"I don't think so."

"Really, you just use proxies and bots to—"

"But I don't think I'm comfortable with—"

"Then fine, don't pawn anything. We can just go, and steal stuff you like—get you a new laptop, so you can finally start designing your own AI instead of just making mods, yeah?" And maybe you'll change your mind when you see what riches these people are hoarding, and decide to go all the way, so you can go to ISU . . . ."

Anya looked almost as distressed as she had right before telling F her scholarship was gone.

"Look at me and tell me you don't deserve a better computer—to have the tools you actually need to do your work," Felix said, the tears spilling out again. "Look at me and honestly tell me that, and if you can, then . . . ."

Anya stared into F's eyes for a while, and her face slowly relaxed. Then, "Can we do it safely?"

Felix had found the house on Red Door, a bnb-like website with stricter membership requirements, aimed at wealthier travelers and homeowners—definitely people with debt, not credit. The place was un-booked (surprise, no one wanted to go to Greatland Iowa for their holiday break), and had been available since the fifteenth. It was out in the countryside, a twenty-minute bike ride from Felix's house.

By the time they turned off the highway, it'd stopped raining and the sun had set. The drive led them through a thicket of trees into a postage-stamp clearing surrounded by forestry. At the center stood a two-story house with an excessively furnished front porch and a stretch of chain link fence visible toward the back.

"What if that's for a dog?" Anya pointed at the fence.

"If there was a dog it would've been mentioned on Red Door," F murmured. "Your mask is slipping some." F pinched the fabric and stretched it up over the bridge of her nose. They both wore scarves wound tight around their faces just below their eyes and skull caps above, in case of security cams.

"Alright," Felix said, taking out F's phone, "I'm gonna call you now."

F walked their bikes over to the side of a long shed catty-corner to the house, then propped F's phone on the handlebars so the camera pointed out to the road.

Anya took out her phone. "So if I see someone drive through here on this call, what do we do?"

"We hide in the trees and wait them out," Felix said. "Private security is not going to *want* to find us, you know? They'll get here, look around the house, and assume we ran away. They're not in the business of catching people, just chasing them off."

"What about police?"

"Police are all in Muscatine helping with the flood, they don't have time for anything happening in pissant little Greatland." F made for the house. "Now come on, let's do this."

They'd cased the place on Google Maps and seen, in a summer picture, little plants set out on the shallow incline of the porch roof. If someone could move plants in and out through the windows, a person could probably make it through too. They'd also discovered that one wall of the porch consisted of a lattice choked with vines, which made for an easy climb up to the awning.

"Look, this is the one," Felix whispered, motioning Anya over to one of the second story windows. Behind the glass, they could see the plants set out on the windowsill. Although it was a pain to remove the screen with their gloves on, the window wasn't actually locked or bolted into place, and it slid up easily.

"Careful with the plants, Felix," Anya said, as Felix squirmed past them.

"No names, Bug," Felix hissed back at her, and as she came in behind F, F went and looked for the light. "You in?" Felix asked.

"Yeah," Anya said, and hearing the window sliding shut, Felix hit the switch.

The room was a bathroom, with two sinks and a closet twice the size of Felix's own, but *just for towels*. The shower/bathtub overflowed with products—conditioner, dry scalp conditioner, scented shampoo, bodywash, a chunky bar of soap, washcloths, a luffa, a glass jar of bath salts—and the counter of the bathroom held even more—shaving cream, razors, more bars of soap, combs, hairbrushes, nail scissors, deodorants, perfume, eyeliner, lip gloss, foundation and setting powder (none the right shade for Anya *or* Felix), mouthwash, toothpaste, an army of orange prescription bottles. Just as stunning as the quantity and variety of the stuff, all of them were name brand. These people were debtors for sure.

As they progressed through an upstairs hallway, then down a flight of stairs to the living room, they followed the same routine. Turn on the lights, survey the area, check in with each other to see if either of them wanted something, then turn off the lights and move on. Felix didn't take much, but Anya wasn't taking anything. "Are you *sure*?" Felix asked. "Something small?" They both wore backpacks that they could stuff a lot of things into. "No," she said, "I don't want their stuff. I'm just looking for a laptop." And on they went.

The house was overstuffed, top to bottom. Even the fridge and pantry were well-stocked, with more animal products in one place than Felix had ever seen outside a supermarket. F used Anya's phone to check the price of a block of cheddar cheese, $31.50. F marked it down on F's tally and took it, instantly tearing open the packaging and taking a big bite. Felix hadn't had dairy cheese since F was six, before the carbon taxes made it too expensive, and it was creamy beyond anything Felix could remember. Rich and dense like a potato, sweet, and salty and fatty like peanut butter. F offered the block to Anya. "Want some?"

"No, I'm vegan. Aren't you vegan?"

"Everyone's vegan," Felix said, taking another bite, really

chewing on it.

"So why are you eating that?"

"It's not like I'm buying it," F said. "And it's delicious. Why not enjoy the fruits of their greed?" Felix wrapped up the cheese and stuck it into F's backpack, quickly following it with a box of cookies that ran about $29, a loaf of sourdough ($19), a jar of blackberry jam ($15), a half-used bag of Sumatra coffee (half of $44—$22), and a small travel mug ($31).

When they reached the home office Anya finally stopped checking her phone every two minutes to pore over the enormous desk at the end of the room, which held two monitors and an enormous computer tower.

F smiled under F's scarf, then turned to the wall opposite the desk where three floor-to-ceiling bookshelves stood. After Felix had raided them, F powered on the computer to calculate how much credit F had left. F didn't want to bother Anya asking her for her phone, as she was now sitting cross-legged on the floor, bent over a Tupperware box full of electronic paraphernalia with that I-am-now-just-in-my-own-world-and-I-don't-care-how-I-look-to-anyone-else concentration that Felix had always found so adorable in her. $563.32—that was how much F was still owed. F was about to shut down the computer when a folder on the desktop caught F's eye.

"Oh my god," Anya whispered, as Felix opened the folder, titled "spreadsheets."

"What?" F looked over, and saw her holding a small, slender laptop.

"This is so new . . . this is just a year old . . . it's a Ryder Mini, it's . . . ." And now, even though her mouth was completely obscured, Felix knew that Anya was smiling.

"How much is it?"

"About five thousand dollars," she said.

"Take it, Bug!"

Anya slung her backpack around the front of her and slipped the laptop inside. "What are you doing?"

Felix's eyes roamed across the screen. "These are quarterly reports, for this family's farm—we could feed this into that personal AI and figure out how much these people owe—we'd know *exactly* how much you can take from them—it's probably enough to pay for college."

"Well, probably," Anya murmured. "But . . . ."

"I'm doing it." Felix opened the web browser and rattled off a search query.

"Fe—I mean, just, those, the AI don't handle businesses very well. They're not optimized for them."

"Really? Because the site has an option for 'business' in this dropdown." Felix selected this option, and then rather than filling out any forms, clicked "Upload Data."

"Huh," Anya said. "Must be a more recent build . . . ."

Felix selected all the folders F'd looked at, plus several more that F hadn't, but which seemed relevant. The AI was smart, it could sort out what was and wasn't important for itself. They both watched as a progress bar appeared on the screen and crawled from 5% to 23% to 29% to 44%, much faster than it would've done on Anya's computer or Felix's. In less than a minute, the bar was up to 99%, and then the page reloaded and the number appeared: $4,344,505.

"What the fuck?" Felix said. "Whoa, what?"

"See, that's what I'm saying, I don't know how accurate—"

"Would it be *this* inaccurate? Really? There's something in that data, this family's done some shit, Anya."

"That's . . . this number is . . . ."

"Slaveholding, or maybe they're descended from some old shitty European dynasty, or—"

"That's not in the data!" Anya snapped. "There's no tab that records the number of slaves this family's ancestors had—and we're in Iowa, these people are probably descended from protestant Germans, not slaveholders or monarchs."

"Then they're paying people below minimum wage, or using some massively pollutant farming process," Felix said. "Either way, their shit is ours for the taking. This room is a great place to start, you tell me, what's valuable in here?"

"F, if *that's* their debt, I, I don't know how much we can trust my credit."

"What? Of course we can, it's consistent with other reparations AI."

"Well, you know, that's an average, it's not like every black person is, has some legacy of deprivations, or—"

"Of course not, but you—your dad's dad's dad's dad was a

slave, right? We can say that with certainty."

"But my mom's white, and I've—I can't deny the benefits of that, or—"

"That is ridiculous, and you know it." Felix picked up an external drive, and unzipped Anya's pack to put it in.

"Stop!" she yelled, spinning away. "I'm saying, I don't feel like I've had some horrible life of being withheld from opportunities, I, I feel incredibly grateful for everything I've got, especially considering what my dad went through, and I don't feel like a hundred thousand dollars has been robbed from me."

"You don't have to feel it." Felix shoved the drive into F's own pack and started grabbing other electronics. "The computer is telling you." F picked up a phone, then realized it was Anya's, which she had left on the desk—but in the moment F picked it up, F saw a shape moving out of frame, toward the house. "Shit! Come on, grab everything as quickly as possible!"

"What, F, is there—" Her voice choked up.

"Yeah, let's go!" F flipped off the lights. "Listen, do these rich assholes deserve these electronics more than you deserve college?"

"I—*No*," she hissed, and she pushed past F and plunged her hands into the box of electronics, fishing out sleek black and gray apparatuses and placing them on the desk by the light of the monitor. Felix helped her, filling up F's own pack as well as hers.

"Wait, F," Anya whispered, staring at the computer monitor.

"What, you want to take that?"

"This isn't the Midwest AI, this is global." Anya looked at F. "This isn't what they owe to the creditors of the Midwest, or America, it's what they owe to the *world*."

"But that's—"

"Why it's so high—someone must've cracked it in the past few days, figured out how to—"

An enormous crashing sound as the front door exploded open, and something came skittering down the hall, knocking off the walls and into the office. The doorknob.

"Whoever is in there," a voice boomed from the doorway, "get the fuck out, and leave your shit!" Not private security. A looter.

There were two exits to the office—one to the front hallway, one to the dining room. If Felix remembered correctly, from the dining room they could get to the backyard—but they'd have to move quick.

"F, look," Anya pointed to the monitor, which displayed the homepage for the site that Felix had breezed past when F was uploading the data. Anya's finger was pressed to a text box which read,

$36,433

Average debt of a lower-class US citizen

"I'll give you till ten to come over here and surrender whatever you've taken!" The voice yelled.

"I've got a plan," Felix hissed. "Out the back."

"One! Two!"

Anya stuck close as they crept through the dining room.

"Three! Four!"

"I hate this," she moaned.

"Five! Six!"

Felix used every shouted number as a chance to open the creaking door further.

"Seven! Eight!"

Across the threshold now . . . .

"Nine! Ten!"

And it was closed. They heard stomping inside and quickly scurried off the back porch to crouch beside some hedges. The rain had come back—no, it was snow this time.

"Okay," Anya said, "what now?"

"Now we sneak around to our bikes and GTFO."

"Wait, that was your plan? Are you serious? No, no, then we should just give the stuff back—"

"Keep your voice down," Felix snapped, and F headed toward the edge of the house.

From inside they heard the looter shout something, and they froze at the corner of the house for a while before continuing on to the chain link fence, which enclosed the backyard. "Let's go over the fence one at a time," F said, "so we don't make too much noise." Felix fit one foot into a hole and, pushing off of it, for the first time that night felt the enormous weight of F's pack. The chains jangled, and F climbed as quickly as possible, easing F's body down to the other side. F could see the bikes from here just yards away, Felix could see F and Anya riding away on them, Felix could see huge sums rolling into Anya's bank account and Felix could see her graduating with F.

"Jesus this is heavy," Anya said, reaching the top of the fence. She sat there, straddling the metal pole running across the top. "I won't be able to bike up and down hills with all this on my back."

There was more shouting in the house. "You can and will," Felix said, "now get down from there!"

Anya pulled down her scarf, one hand still clasping the fence for balance. "I can't, Felix . . . I, you saw what that site said—none of this is ours. I mean, if we really want to be accountableist, we should donate our *own* things to, to displaced Indonesians—or to Puerto Ricans, or—"

"We're just kids!" Felix said. "We can do all that later, once we've gotten an education and have jobs that—"

"I know you want us to go the same university, but—"

"That's not what this is about!" Felix shouted, then instantly clapped a hand over F's mouth. In the silence, Anya began slipping off her pack with her free hand.

Felix reached up to snatch it, but Anya twisted away. "If you let go of that," Felix said, "you're letting go of everything that's been stripped away from your ancestors for generations—you're letting go of—" F swiped at it again.

"You don't get to steal on behalf of my ancestors!" Anya hissed. The pack now hung by just one strap, which she reached for.

"*I'm* not stealing it, it's not *mine*, it's for *you*, when you come to your senses!" Just as Anya took hold of the strap Felix jumped up to grab it. F caught onto her scarf instead and without a thought yanked as hard as possible, sending scarf, Anya, and backpack tumbling over the fence and slamming into the hard cold ground.

Felix stared in horror. "Oh my—Anya, Bug, I didn't—I'm sorry, I—"

Anya pushed herself up. "Fucking take it, asshole," she said, shoving the pack into F's hands. "I don't want it."

"But the laptop—"

"Fuck the laptop. Slave labor pollutant bullshit anyway." She walked past F, then froze.

"Hand it over!"

F turned and saw the looter heading toward them. As they got closer, Felix could see a handgun tucked into the waistband of their jeans. "My buddy in the car heard you idiots. What'd you think, I came alone?" Though their face was covered by a ski mask, they sounded young, maybe early twenties.

"What's, what's your credit tally?" Felix asked, voice shaking. "Why do you deserve this more than her?" The looter stopped a few yards away from them, and Anya backed up to stand in front of Felix. "She needs this money for college."

"College? Fuck off," the looter said. "Give me the bags."

Felix chucked over F's own bag, still holding onto Anya's pack. "You'd just take a girl's education from her? She deserves a—"

"Kid, unless she's a Rohingya or some shit, she doesn't deserve dick. Looting isn't about deserving, it's about wanting. If you prefer to use a credit tally, whatever. But my credit tally's only twenty-k. Fuck that. I want a car, I want a treadmill, I want some weed and I want a flat screen and a VR system and I want a big motherfuckin' hamburger, and I want that goddamn backpack, now." The looter's hand had come to rest on their handgun. Felix held out Anya's bag, and the looter took it. "Community college is cheap enough anyway, she'll be fine." They then grabbed Felix's bag off the ground.

"Don't take that," Anya spoke up. "There's a few electronics on top, you can take those, but the rest is just books and some food."

The looter, putting on Anya's backpack, unzipped Felix's and upended it, shaking it out vigorously. After a moment's consideration of the pile of takings, they cast the empty bag aside and stood back up. "I don't want any of that shit." They turned and headed back to the house.

"Do you treat most looters like this?" Felix asked. "Why can't we work together? We're on the same side!"

"Yeah kid," the looter called back. "We're the *debtors.*" They disappeared from sight then, but F heard a car door slam, and after a while the front door of the house opening and closing.

Felix picked up F's backpack as Anya walked away toward the bikes, and F looked at all the items scattered in the snow and dead leaves. Books and electronics that weren't F's. What the fuck was F doing with someone else's food?

F arranged the petty plunder in a neat stack by the side of the house, using the heavier items to weigh down the flimsier ones. F put on the empty backpack and walked to the bikes, spying someone inside the looter's car who watched F back. When Felix had biked out to the edge of the property, F was surprised to almost come crashing into Anya, who was standing on the edge of the highway beside her bike.

Felix pulled down F's scarf. "You deserve the world," F said to her. "You deserve everything, nothing could be enough."

Anya didn't respond.

"You'll still do great, even without going to a big university. I'm the one who's going to be struggling, without, without . . . ." A cold wind whipped through F. "I'm so sorry. I know an apology isn't enough, I owe you so much more—"

"Can I have my phone?" Anya said.

"Your . . . ."

"When you saw the car come in, you took my phone," Anya said.

"I . . . ." Felix felt F's stomach roll. "I put it in your bag. I can, I'll go back and—"

"No," Anya said, "don't be reckless."

"Then—then you can have *my* phone, please, let me—"

"*No.* Just text my phone, letting the looters know I'd like it back. And give them your number so they can work it out with you. It's a cheap phone. They won't mind not keeping it, and if they do it won't be expensive to replace."

"Oh—okay." Felix nodded, and Anya got on her bike and kicked back the stand.

"Hey, what's the credit tally needed for snow?" she said, then pushed off down the road.

For the first time, Felix realized, truly took account of the fact, that it was snowing. It was snowing, in Iowa, in December no less. F couldn't remember the last time that'd happened—maybe before F was born.

The credit tally needed for snow. More than Greatland deserved. More than Middle America, agricultural heart of a miserly old debtor empire, deserved. More than Felix deserved, too, idiot. But it was falling on F, anyway.

Francis Bass is an undergraduate student at the University of Iowa, though he is a native of Tallahassee, Florida. His work has appeared in *Dramatics* magazine and the *Thespian Playworks 2014* anthology, and he has self-published several short stories and plays. You can find him online at francisbass.com.

The Invasion of Yonkers: People and Plants

Mansuda Arora

The city of Yonkers is being invaded in many different ways at once.

Among the types of invasive plants that plague Westchester county are Kudzu, Mile-a-Minute, Oriental Bittersweet, Porcelain Berry, Multiflora Rose, Purple Loosestrife and Japanese Knotweed. Each has a distinct personality; they can be identified by leaf shape, size, color and the aggression and speed with which they spread. One learns to hate certain species more than others. I've spent countless hours removing Multiflora thorns from my fingertips. My muscles have become stiff from cutting vines that have grown thicker than a baby's arm. My skin is raised and itchy from contact with poison ivy and oak. My back is sore from pulling weeds rooted so deeply that the earth puts up a fight releasing them.

A species is classified as invasive when it is not only foreign but has no local predators, meaning that it can spread prolifically without being eaten, siphoning resources like space, light, and water from native plant life. Many of these species were brought from Asia by European traders as decorative additions to gardens or church hats. Others came in the hulls of ships along with food and other supplies. Others came as seeds nestled in the hair of slaves. Whatever their origin, they now grow unperturbed along the Saw Mill River and its surrounding trails and forests.

I work with high school students in Yonkers on vine removal and ecology education. We must be careful; my supervisors remind me to stay away from words like "alien" or "invader" because they may be triggering to immigrant students and their families. Instead we are encouraged to use the terms "native" and "non-native". My boss suggests going as far as referring to them within the framework of "colonizers" vs "natives".

The Yonkers city government cannot afford to take on the removal of invasive plants, so it is up to volunteer groups to resist their spread. At volunteer events, I explain that a tree covered in vines may appear to be alive due to the green tendrils that wrap endlessly around its branches, while underneath the thing has been dead for quite some time. This is dangerous because it leaves the tree unstable. Dead branches can fall unexpectedly at any time.

There are very few green spaces left in Yonkers. The small community gardens that litter South West Yonkers are built on city property and are liable to be taken back for "development". Half of these plots are in the process of being converted into luxury condos.

There is no point protesting the uprooting of the gardens in Yonkers. Their removal became inevitable when a new kind of invaders began growing downtown. They take the form of real estate developers and artists escaping the rising price of living in Manhattan and Brooklyn. Like a vine climbing a tree, they tear down affordable housing projects and uproot community gardens to make room for juice bars and upscale art galleries. We are reminded each day that this land does not belong to the community and never will. Every attempt at purchasing the land has been shot down, even when the asking value is met. We are forced to face the reality that money makes money and community gardens do not.

There is still trash in the river, protest over the removal of trees, miles of invasive plants that grow faster than we can cut them, and rising property taxes as a result of cleaning up the city that belongs to the community who can no longer afford to live there. We spend the day digging up the garden on Buena Vista Avenue that is older than any of us to make room for a parking lot; it can get discouraging. Buena Vista literally means "good view", and we all recognize the irony when the new apartment complexes have been blocking the view of the Hudson for months.

To be young and of color, a child of an immigrant, is to be a product of "outreach", surrounded by community, on land you do not own, in a city full of abandoned spaces still teeming with life. Having been touched by white systems if not white people—until they leave their hometowns—the kids I work with are happy simply with opportunity, the opportunity to fail, even. Failure rarely has anything to do with their own shortcomings but centuries and tons and miles of circumstance. I know they will blame themselves anyway, and work hard like our parents and grandparents and great grandparents, all while praying that they never end up like them. When the parents ask, *"Why are you doing this again?"* we are reminded that our parents did not *"come to this country to have you picking fruit".*

Humans are the deadliest of invasive species, our vines growing ever upward, blocking precious sunlight.

We must become environmentalists. It is our obligation.

I'm talking about a second definition of environmentalism as well as the first: not only *concern about and action aimed at protecting the environment,* but *the theory that environment, as opposed to heredity, has the primary influence on the development of a person or group.*[1]

I understand wanting to leave when it feels like there is less and less space for the community to occupy; when they tell you your music is too loud; no, you cannot skate here; your art is vandalism; it's past curfew; this is city property; no loitering; this area is under surveillance by camera.

In a city of immigrants, some documented, some not, the issue of invasion is blurry. Who is the invader on land that belongs to the Lene Lenape tribe, whose presence can be felt if not seen? None of us are native to this land. Whether we immigrated from overseas and beyond borders or were brought here against our will, we are all here now.

A community deserves land for themselves that cannot be taken away, occupied or invaded. A place to grow for the sake of growing rather than the sake of profit. A place with enough space, sunlight and water to thrive. But right now, the city of Yonkers is being invaded, and it doesn't look like we are going to be able to stop it.

Along any highway in Westchester county, the invasion is evident. If you take the time to look, nearly every surface is covered in the relentless vines. They elicit a visceral reaction from me now, a feeling of rage and anxiety that lives in my chest. Deep down I believe that the task of removing them is impossible, but I will never say this aloud. Invasive removal has become a kind of therapy to work out a whole list of anxieties I cannot speak aloud for fear that speaking them into existence will make them real, that my community and

---

1 Oxford Living Dictionaries

communities like it do not stand a chance of thriving under these conditions. Still, I go out each week and work, little by little, in the hopes that I am very wrong.

Mansuda Zeba Arora is a writer, activist and educator living in Yonkers, New York. She is the co-editor and chief of *Dark Phrases*, the oldest literary magazine run by students of color in the U.S. She is currently a senior at Sarah Lawrence College.

Paddling in the Sound

Adelia MacWilliam

Not long after the election, when the left had failed
to reassure the broken hearted,
and the broken hearted had elected a lunatic
out of spite, I kayaked out to where the light
had never been torn,
to watch the darkness gathering
in the mountains' seams.

Cool rain on flat seas, ducks ahead of me,
white trails of their wings beating water
as they fled. Fresh scent of snow in the wind.

A loon in the distance
began to call again and again,
a soliloquy from the sea's grey throat,
each note going deeper into
where a certainty had once lived in my heart.

The longing in the loon's call—a knife
cutting through rain, leaving nothing behind it
but more longing, more rain.

Adelia MacWilliam recently completed her MFA in poetry at the University of Victoria advised by Homer Award winning poet Tim Lilburn. She wrote about a piece of land on Salt Spring Island that her family had "occupied" since 1905 and learned that if you cast the mythic imagination across a piece of land that has always been part of your life, everything will out. She is co-founder of Cascadia Poetics Lab, which produces the annual Deep In Cascadia poetry events in Cumberland, and the monthly Red Tree reading series. She spends her time between Cumberland and Desolation Sound.

A Diary from the End of the World

Cécile Cristofari

Worlds depart; their light endures.

Over five years before, I had arrived on the planet we call DA3(1), the Third Daughter of star Alkahran and the only life-bearing body in the system. As with most planets, this one had no specific name in the language of its natives: they called their sun the Sun, their world the World, and its inhabitants People. This world was not dying, but signs of the extinction of its dominant species were already there: squeezed between a voracious and utterly unviable relationship to their habitat and a generalised sense of doom, the people of DA3(1) might yet recover, or they might not. The savants of the galaxy already mentioned them with the tinge of regret reserved for disappearing beauty. Recording the glow from their fading embers was the perfect job for an exoethnologist, and so I was given an assignment there, to gather as much as I could of their culture in case it was lost forever.

I had spent the past few months in a place called Montevideo, sipping *mate* tea from a gourd and adding sketches of parakeet vendors to a string of unsorted field notes, when the mental call from Brood Mother came.

'The Grand Central Reactors have failed for good,' she said, her voice shaking with more than interferences from stellar winds.

The implications did not reach my brain at once. It takes longer to form an adequate reaction when you have transformed your body into one of another species, and for a moment, all I could think of was the warm *mate* cup in my hand and how annoying it was to be unable to receive space transmissions properly.

'We have to evacuate,' Brood Mother said. 'Me, your sisters, we all have to leave. They say it's hopeless. There will never been enough fuel to start them again.'

I put the cup down. In the dying throes of our sun, the Grand Central Reactors were all that kept the cold at bay. If we had only known they would run out of energy so fast . . . .

'How long is there left?' I said.

'A month or so. We can't be sure. Please, daughter . . . please come back.'

I blinked. My eyes, native eyes in a native body I had composed five years before, suddenly seemed to remember the soft red light of my own sun, and the glare of DA3(1) blinded me. Getting near my ship would be simple enough: air transportation operated all over this planet. It was the last few dozen kilometres that worried me. I had left my transporter hidden on a remote island to make sure it would come to no harm, but that meant it would be days, at best, before I could reach it.

'I'll be there, Brood Mother,' I quickly said before she could sense my uncertainty.

There are thousands of records of worlds ending, but I had never seen anything quite like the place they called World's End in Tierra del Fuego: a colourful city sprawled between mountains still capped with snow, with the sea glistening greyish blue some distance away. Boats swayed in the port under a weak breeze: mostly travellers, people of means and wanderlust, with little need for extra crew. It might take days before I found someone to take me to the other end of the Beagle channel, through its maze of islands, to where the transporter waited for me.

It was a strange city, Ushuaia, a place where no one seemed to linger, and yet where everyone appeared to come seeking a truth of some sort. End of the World, it said everywhere, as if it was a great thing. I sat in a café full of tourists in expensive hiking gear, like a very expensive interstellar tourist myself.

I tried listening to the conversations around me, out of habit. But there was little I managed to record. After five years on another planet, in another body, taking notes on everything until it became second nature, all I could now think about was a reddish sky illuminated by a huge sun, with purple trees bending in the wind.

I finally embarked upon a sturdy steel-hulled schooner manned by three Frenchmen—a sailor, a violinist, and a biologist, who taught me about birds in between bouts of peering at seawater through a microscope. Less than two days into our voyage, there was already no trace of human occupation left around us. Glaciers dropped into the sea from black, naked mountaintops. Flocks of penguins, albatrosses and petrels fled before us, inaudible with the whistle of the wind in the halyards. Aside from these and the occasional sea lion surfacing like a black blot in the distance, there was no animal presence, although many beasts roamed the depths of the sea, my companions had assured me. I had never seen the near-mythical beast they called a whale, but around here, those animals were undisputed queens.

On my home world, there were very few places so entirely devoid of people.

'Hasn't anyone ever lived here?' I asked.

'They used to, yes. They were slaughtered.'

I remembered encountering countless black-and-white pictures in Ushuaia of a long-gone people wrapped in furs and staring at the camera with nostalgia. Their names, Selknam, Yaghan, Haush, Kawésqar, were mentioned with reverence. Nowhere did anyone allude to the fact that they had been exterminated in less than a century to make room for cattle and fishing boats.

We'd had our genocides at home too. We did not like discussing them in the open either, and I could only suppose that now the end had come, most people would prefer to feel sorry for themselves and forget past guilt. That was how it seemed to be happening on DA3(1), at any rate.

'Would you like a sip?' my biologist companion offered, handing me the *mate* cup, once the waves calmed down a little.

It was a welcome respite from thinking. We sat together in the cockpit, enjoying a few minutes of warmth from the tiny, bright yellow sun.

'You're very silent,' one of them observed. 'Is everything fine?'

It was. It had to be. The panicked call this morning from Brood Mother was nothing; you would expect her to feel nervous in a time like this, and I was going to the transporter as fast as I could. I had acquired a decent command of most of this species' expressions by then, so my broad smile reassured them.

'Penguins,' I said, pointing out to the now-quiet waters of the channel. 'Look.'

As the ship approached, the tiny, black-and-white shapes dropped one by one into the waters. I gazed at a massive ice field cascading into the sea, surrounded by smooth rock where the ice had retreated. When I was a hatchling, my brood used to worry about the ice creeping up to our village, not away from it. I grew up to dread the sight of ice. Yet for some reason, with two hundred metres of cold, dark water under the hull and steep banks covered in impassably convoluted trees on either side of the channel, the situation felt peaceful, comforting.

The loss of an intelligent species is not the end of the world, I reminded myself. It was hard to keep that truth in mind sometimes. If humans disappeared from DA3(1), this place would hardly change at all.

Three days in, we approached the other side of the channel.

'We could see whales around here,' my biologist friend said. 'We're close enough to the ocean, and the waters are deep. I hope we'll see them.' He grinned like a child, a hand on the rigging to steady himself as he half-hung above the water—two hundred metres of kelp and darkness and massive wandering beasts.

'Everybody seems fascinated with whales,' I remarked.

'They should be. Whales are as intelligent as we are. Just imagine, we could learn their language one day! How cool is that?'

I thought he was joking, but his grin was one of excitement, not of irony.

'I thought you—' I checked myself. 'I thought *we* were the only intelligent species on this planet?'

'Lots of species are intelligent,' he retorted. 'They just don't write books about it.'

I had never thought of it this way, not even back home. I

stared into the depth. But the water was so dark you couldn't see anything one metre below the surface. I realised that, after five years on DA3(1), I knew next to nothing about whales, or any other species for that matter. Perhaps I had talked with too few biologists.

There were few whales left, my friend said, but this was one of a few places on Earth where they regularly came to hunt. Now I thought about it, on the day I had landed, I had seen a dark shape rise over the surface of the water and sink back down in a couple of seconds. I had not known about whales back then, although I had taken time to study local cultures through the haphazard messages they sent to outer space.

'I hope we'll see whales too,' I said, to keep my thoughts from straying towards those years when I studied exoethnology from the comfort of my doomed home.

The sea spread like a sheet of metal ahead, so smooth the reflections looked as vivid as the mountains themselves. I gazed in the distance for the tapping of albatross feet in the waves, waters poked open by the back of a Chilean dolphin, or perhaps even a tall plume of spray that would announce the coming of a whale. The rumble of the motor blurred all other sounds, isolating hearing more than silence itself. But the broadcast echoing in my head bypassed exterior noise.

'It's over,' Brood Mother said.

I did not answer for a moment. I was taking the news surprisingly well. I was not sure how the body I had adopted was supposed to react, but so far it hardly seemed to react at all.

'You said there would be a month left,' I said.

'They ordered evacuation today. It's over. We won't ever come back.'

She said more things afterwards; that we had always known after all; that my sisters were not adjusting badly, all things considered; that the barracks on GDKZ5-3 were clean and pleasant. She did not say how our planet looked as the spaceship soared away. I imagined it would have shrunk to the size of a ball, then a tiny, cold silver pebble, alone and dying in the emptiness.

Something warm started to flow from my eyes, as if, of its own accord, my borrowed body knew about the beauty of the lakes on my home world at moonrise, the bellows of the storms in the trees, the cries of river birds in the morning. Water ran down my cheeks, so familiar after five years of use, yet so foreign in that moment. I tried to push myself out, to throw my mind towards the transporter however I could and fly away I didn't know where. But grief tore my focus apart. I'd have to reach the transporter before I could get away from the form I had adopted, and so I stayed there, clutching the rigging, trying to remain motionless even as my mind cracked piece by piece.

There was a hesitant touch on my arm.

'Are you all right?' one of the crew asked. I forced my face into stillness.

'I. . . .' My voice croaked. I blurted out the first justification that would not sound too strange to them. 'It's . . . the anniversary. Today. My mother's death.'

I did not turn to face him, but I received his words nonetheless. They were kind and awkward and brief. People here did not know how to deal with endings. He walked away soon and they left me alone, respecting a grief they understood so much less than they thought.

Island after island, channel after channel, the labyrinth unfolded towards the edge of the Pacific Ocean.

I did not discuss my supposed mourning any further with the crew. Instead I asked them about whales. I asked about whale song and what calves might learn from their mothers; whales helping out other beasts although nobody knew why; whales giving each other names; whales staying behind when hunted so that their pod members would not die alone; whales approaching ships without fear and being slaughtered for their flesh, even though nobody ate it anymore. We talked about albatrosses and penguin families and the tiny passerines that flocked to see what curious sorts of beasts we were when we neared the shore and shut down the motor. We talked and talked, warming our hands on *mate* cups and sipping the bitter warmth of the tea with delight, but we hardly looked at one another. Our eyes remained riveted on the blue and white humps of the mountains around us, the silver stillness of the sea.

Once, as we passed a waterfall gushing from under a glacier, I said—

'There was a river near our house, when I was a child. And a waterfall, just like this one.'

My biologist friend nodded gravely and let me go on. So I told him about cold mornings bathed in red dawns, and taking walks near the water to pick tart little berries in woods rustling with beasts he knew no name for. I told him how I heard the voices of my grandmother and aunts in the wind and he smiled, no doubt thinking I meant it as a metaphor. I did not tell him about the daily reports on the central reactors that kept the core of our planet warm even after the warmth of the sun had failed it — about peacefully waiting for an ending everybody thought they would accept without question, as if we would always be able to hear the voice of our world and of our dead sun in the galactic wind.

I heard my own voice splinter before I felt it in my throat. I stopped talking.

My friend looked away and pointed at the shape of a sea lion, to give me a moment of privacy.

'We lived in a house by the sea when I was little,' he suddenly said.

I remembered what I had learned about warming climate and rising sea levels on DA3(1).

'Is it still there?' I asked.

He nodded.

'It's not going anywhere,' he replied. 'It's just that there are more storms now. It gets flooded more and more often, and it won't get better. I haven't been there in a while.'

He did not sound as buoyant as he usually did, and I did not insist. But his smile came back after a brief silence, as he told me about a childhood on the beach, glimpsing octopuses and hermit crabs in beds of seagrass, eating bitter red berries from trees that grew short and dense in the salt seaside heat. The more I listened, the more I seemed to hear another voice under that of the seasoned sailor: the voice of an excited little boy reading about fish and dolphins, running on a beach and lecturing his family about the cuttlefish bones and seashells he found there, building up a steadfast love of the sea when everybody thought he was just playing. I remembered lying down in the grass and gazing at the stars, revelling in the certainty that there were other worlds to explore even as the first reports of alien probes reaching our orbit were broadcast. Without the strange shape of his limbs and face, this alien could have been a sister of mine.

'It will stay there,' I said. 'None of it is going away.'

But I was not sure what I was talking about.

I recognised the shape of the island even though it looked exactly like all the islands around. It was the first thing I had seen of this world after landing, the place where I had left the transporter five years before.

But the familiar pulsing noise at the back of my head was absent. Aside from the song of the halyards against the masts, there was nothing to be heard. I reached with my thoughts. The body I had adopted was less sensitive than my native one. But there was no sound even as we neared the island. When I tried to empty my mind, I could not find the familiar echo. It was as if my own heart had stopped beating.

I stood still on the side of the ship as the realisation dawned on me. The transporter was in constant contact with installations on my home world. There would have been no reason to keep them running as evacuation neared completion. Without its transgalactic anchor, my ship could not function. It lay there inactive, dead as the world that had made it.

I would never be able to go back.

Hours passed and I still stood gazing at the island, probing with my mind even when I knew there would be no answer. Far ahead, the islands grew farther apart, the wind and waves more insistent. To a sailing ship, the passage to the open ocean was trickier than crossing half the universe had been to me. But when would my people start exploring the galaxy again if they had a whole world to rebuild?

I was alone, and stranded, and even if I ever found a way to go back, there was no 'back' anymore. I would only land in yet another new world, one where I would speak my native tongue and where people looked familiar again, but where the rustle of the trees and the smells and tastes and bird songs would never be the same.

As I desperately reached into the silence, a hollow sound burst through the sea, immediately followed by shouts. I jerked back to the ship as the sailors rushed to the prow.

A huge shape broke the water, shiny and black, its blowhole visible for a second, then the length of its back, then the tail unfolding out of the water and sinking again, as large as my entire body, not twenty metres from the ship. The sound of its blow had split the air like a horn, but it sank soundlessly, while the crew whooped and ran across the ship in hope to see it surface again. But in the wasteland of my mind reaching out for a signal that would never come, another sound rushed like a wave, the echo of a mind bigger and deeper than any I had ever encountered—

Little one little calf on the water hurt are you hurt I am here little one I will help . . . .

I stepped on the bowsprit, as far as I could, a strange feeling of weightlessness washing over me, as if I had reached the transporter and was changing into my native form again. I spread my mind open. Concern, gentle worry for a strange creature flooded my thoughts, and I probed for a way to respond, *no hurt I'm fine I'm fine stay please stay here . . . .*

The sound of the blow echoed again amid cries of wonder, and perhaps I saw the whale surface again, although sight and thought were too mingled to tell apart. Amid hissing waves and grey summits, I let myself drift for the last time, letting go of my borrowed body and perhaps of my native one as well, too far away from the safety of the transporter to know how it would end, and too far gone to care. The shouts of wonder turned to cries of warning, but overlaying my senses came the vast drifting thoughts again, *little creature little stranger I will help you hurt no hurt you're safe you're safe . . . .*

My feet lost the bowsprit, but there was no cold to meet me. I greeted the water like a long-lost home, I felt my mind change into one I had never imagined, and just before I lost words to enter a never-ending song, I realised that I was swimming home, in the only place in the universe where the world was not ending.

To *Sonate* and her crew: Robin Cristofari, Florian Maury and Jean-Christophe Gairard.

Cécile Cristofari lives in South France, where she teaches English to unruly but endearing teenagers. Her stories have previously appeared in *Daily Science Fiction.* She blogs at http://staywherepeoplesing.wordpress.com/

Cliff Projection

Feral X

Feral X is a guerilla projectionist based in the UK. Find more of their work at feralx.com.

Feral X was inspired by the work of the New York based arts collective, The Illuminator, whose website incorporates a helpful tip sheet on the equipment needed to set up your own guerrilla projection project.

Having purchased a projector, caravan battery, inverter and linked them up to a laptop and messed around with the equipment until it worked, it was now time to try it out on the street.

The Feather Wall

Octavia Cade

Dog would eat anything. That was a comfort. If Martin had had to starve the poor bugger he might have thought twice about keeping quarantine, because the only other alternative was unacceptable. At some point, hunger would likely have pushed Dog to break his training and go for the kakapo, and the two of them had worked too hard on Resolution to see that happen.

There were staples enough in the ranger hut to last the season, if he stretched them, but no chance of restocking from the mainland any time soon. He checked the radio every day, calling out in case the plague was over, in case anyone had survived, but there was never any answer. Perhaps that meant it was safe to go back, perhaps the thing had burnt itself out, but if it hadn't . . . .

Martin wouldn't have minded if it had just been himself. It wouldn't be much of a life anyway, the last man alone or as good as, at the arse-end of the world where no-one was likely to come along. There'd be no-one left behind to grieve for him but Dog, and even knowing that he'd laid awake at night, stroking the soft head and wondering if a bullet wouldn't be kinder. He promised himself he'd do it, if he felt the sickness on him. Better a quick end at the hand of the human who loved him than slow starvation and loneliness.

He dreamed of it sometimes.

Sickness on him, and sweat. Huddled in his bunk, and in his dream he could never find the gun and Dog was by him always, pressed against him, trying to keep warm and comfort. Growing thinner over the days, because Dog would never leave his human to try and find food, no matter how much Martin cursed him away and tried to make him go. Dog's ribs like toast racks against him, and the fever burning him up until it broke.

Dog licking the salt off his face and that face getting less red and less wet. Dog going to sleep beside him, curled in a hard and bony ball, pushing his nose under Martin's hand. Dog waking to the sensation of cold weight against him, and no pat.

Dog nudging him and whining, Dog taking his fur between his teeth and pulling, Dog licking a face that wasn't warm any more . . . .

The dreams came often, and less often when he checked the gun of a night, placed it carefully under the bed so that it was in easy reach if ever he lost strength enough so that he couldn't even walk across the room. That was how it happened, he'd heard. The quiet incubation period, the sudden loss of strength. Massive contagion, massive mortality, and him and Dog away from it all, on an island they tried to keep predator-free because there was such a thing as conservation even now, and the kakapo would have died without it.

He'd always loved them, dozy as they were: giant flightless parrots on islands full of flightless birds, fat and plentiful until the people came. And the moa died, and the takahe nearly, the kiwi and the kakapo close to as well. Bad enough the human hunters all too eager to take kakapo for trophies, but the daft things couldn't stand against what the humans brought with them—rats and cats and ferrets, creatures that could stalk the kakapo to its burrow and make an end of it, and did so in their thousands. Their tens of thousands, until only a handful remained, and two dozen of those on Resolution.

The island was a good enough place for stragglers to wait out the end times—the ranger's hut was small but well-insulated. It needed to be, because the weather was always shit and Martin didn't know why they'd bothered to put solar panels on the roof because there was never any bloody sunshine anyway, but there was an axe and plenty of wood and he cut some every day, enough to see him through the night and some put away for winter. There was cookware and bunks, a table, a fireplace. Water enough nearby and a tank for storage, a dunny out the back. He could dig a new one when it filled. A few books, not that he was much of a reader, but they'd belonged to one of the other rangers and so had the fishing kit, and he'd made more use of that.

Apocalypse was nothing like Martin thought it would be. Not that he'd ever given it a great deal of brain space, the only times he'd really considered it were superficial ones and in response to a movie usually, or a book. In those the problems were always resources, and he'd always felt a certain sense of smugness at the trouble and conflict it caused. Armed groups scavenging supplies from a local supermarket, warfare over water . . . it all seemed hysterical to him, and not the funny hysterical either. The land was easy enough to live off if you knew what you were doing, and he did.

The angler's kit was basic enough but the water was full of hapuka, of blue cod and gurnard, blue nose and blue-fin. He was able to keep himself and Dog fed, and he knew enough about the local vegetation to keep scurvy at bay. That was how the sailors did it, back when Captain Cook was exploring New Zealand. Back in 1773 it was, in Dusky Sound which was only a stone's throw from Resolution, really. He'd brewed up rimu leaves for a sort of spruce beer, old Cook, but it had been too bitter and so he'd added manuka leaves to soften the flavour. It wasn't exactly craft—Martin found it a bit foul, really, and even Dog didn't do much more than sniff at it, but it was better than loose teeth and open sores, a deficiency of vitamins.

It wasn't keeping himself alive that was the central problem of apocalypse. It wasn't even loneliness, he'd found, because he had Dog and the kakapo, and it wasn't a life for social butterflies anyway, ranging. The Department of Conservation had enough isolated huts that there was always room for rangers to spend weeks, months sometimes, with little enough for company but other DOC rangers, the odd tramper. There'd been two others on Resolution with him, but they'd had families, and at the first radioed hint of trouble they'd left, had promised to come back when it was over.

It was over, and they hadn't come back. Martin was pretty sure their promises hadn't been broken on a whim.

No. The worst thing about apocalypse—and he'd had some weeks now to think it over—wasn't food or change or abandonment. It was loss of purpose.

Martin was under no illusion. Most people, back when there were enough people to make "most" an adequate descriptor, didn't have any sort of lofty goal. It was get through the day mostly, pay the bills, raise the kids if you had them. Be a good mate, maybe leave things a little better than you found them. And if that was a small purpose it was a good one, or good enough. It was the same kind of thinking that sneered at small purpose that made hysteria the primary response to apocalypse, he thought.

"We're an operatic bloody species," he said to Dog. "Always so convinced there's a need for high drama. That it's best, that it's living."

Dog's tail thumped against the wooden floor as if he understood. He probably did too, Martin reckoned, because dogs were pretty operatic themselves, and he'd certainly seen Dog get all over excitement at the prospect of bones.

Now that his purpose was smaller than ever—catch some more fish, feed self, feed Dog, check the radio—it still seemed good. It was that which kept him tethered to Resolution.

"Oh, there's fear in it too," he said to Dog, out of habit more than anything, and because there was always comfort in a good listener. Dog was the best listener that he knew, and the most intelligent. He could spot a lie, could Dog, and Martin liked to work things out with him because it was difficult to look into those intelligent eyes and lie. "I'm not a brave man," he said. "I'm no bloody hero, mate. It's easier to believe people are still out there than to go look and find otherwise. And what would I find, eh?" Corpses, probably. Lots of them, and madness to follow no doubt. "Oh, I'd hold it together. Check it out and come back here, probably, hunker down. And spend the rest of my nights dreaming about what I found, and what I couldn't change."

He dreamed enough about that, and Resolution comforted him because there were things there he could change, still.

It was the kakapo kept him there. And maybe that was his own little streak of operatic, right there, the lone man holding out against inevitability, but he'd heard the booming come back to Resolution, and it made the large things seem possible, somehow. He heard it at night. Short deep bursts, the sound made when blowing over the mouth of a beer bottle. Not all of the males were booming—he could only distinguish two or three of them—and there was no guarantee that any of the females would respond to the mating call, but it was better than silence. "Used to be a time you could walk through Fiordland and hear the booming from every corner," he said to Dog. But that was long before his time, long before his granddad's even. Only old stories now, about how kakapo had been plentiful, and there'd been a time when he'd hoped his work would be one step on the road to making them so again, but apocalypse had put paid to all that.

The other predator-free islands, Codfish and Little Barrier . . . there was no guarantee that any other ranger survived, no reason to think they'd stayed on the islands if they had. Martin had no family left, but most people did; they might have left to go to them like his mates on Resolution had. No guarantee, either, that the predators would stay off them, that one day a clinging rat wouldn't wash up and go hunting for eggs. All the work would mean nothing then. It'd only be a matter of time. And the rats would be growing—a population explosion come from feeding on the bodies of the dead. Possums, as well, with the pest control down to nil and an entire country full of starving pets looking to decimate what was left of the birds. Feral moggies, feral dogs.

He dreamed of it sometimes.

Dog coming back to the hut of a night, limping, scrawny. Dog coming to sit beside remains that wouldn't answer—Dog drooling, sometimes, but he never dreamed of being eaten, of his remains going down that friendly gullet. Partly because the thought of what would happen to his body didn't bother him, even in waking hours, and partly because he shied away from thinking how Dog would need to be, how lost and starved and desperate, before he began to feed.

He was a good mate, was Dog. If Martin died he'd be a last resort—something to be devoured only if Dog was too weak or too sick to catch his own food, and maybe not even then.

But mostly it was because there was something more horrifying to dream about than his own dead self, and that was dead kakapo. He dreamed it near every night—Dog, overcoming training before love, and his mouth stuffed full of parrot. And all the parrots gone, eventually, because they could never escape Dog, stupid feathery things that they were, all whiskers and no brain, and he'd been trained to hunt them down.

That was their tragedy. Kakapo could never escape anything.

Funny, that. In most places the sudden absence of humans would be a shot in the arm to ecosystems. No more poaching, no more pollution. The climate might even get a chance to stabilise—that'd be a good thing. But here and there would be species, remnant populations, dependent on intervention, on protection. "What's going to happen to them, mate?" he said, stroking Dog's floppy ears, and Dog gazed up at him, eyes closing under strokes. "What's going to happen to the kakapo without us to look after them?"

A matter of time only. He knew it, and it wasn't enough to make him go away. He knew every one of those two dozen birds. Knew them all by name, knew their personalities, the way they'd waddle up to him for attention and bits of treat, their great green faces trusting, wistful. Resolution gave him a duty and a purpose, and if apocalypse had taken everything else it hadn't taken that.

Martin wasn't a religious man, but he'd come to feel as an anchorite might, he thought. Wedded to a place, to a purpose, a world made small and the knowledge that there might be someone, someday, who would come and take their place. Maybe. "Too much for us, eh?" he said to Dog. Matters of faith were beyond him. He preferred tools he could hold in his hand: the axe, the traps. Nothing prayerful about them, they were simple and they worked.

It wasn't a difficult job. Meticulous, yes, because he had to check the traps every day, make sure there was nothing in them and reset them if there was. Mostly there was nothing. That was lucky in a way, but it always made Martin wonder if rats had made it back to Resolution and had simply avoided the traps. He set out as many as he could, spent the evening light building more from odd bits of plank, from leftover wire and hinges. But mostly he relied on Dog. They tramped Resolution together, he and Dog. When he'd caught enough fish for the day he'd cook some up, leave the rest for dinner and they'd head off walking.

Dog's nose was better than all the traps combined, and a good thing too. Martin saw the telltale behaviour one afternoon, the whine and hunting pose, and they were off through the bush, slower than he would have liked, for it was mud all through after rain, and it always rained on Resolution. He tripped and slipped behind Dog, gun slung over one shoulder, hoping for a clean end. If it was a stoat, if it was a ferret, and he couldn't find it before dark there'd be no guarantee the kakapo would last the night. Not all of them, anyway, for the mustelids had a blood wish, sometimes, and killed more than they could eat for the sheer pleasure of the killing. Kakapo, big and plump in their burrows, wouldn't be a challenge. He'd find them cold in their entranceways, the beautiful feathers dull and the features uncomprehending. "Find it, Dog!" he cried, mud all down his front and his waterproofs all slick with rain. "Find it!"

Dog was muddy too, his fur damp and with rivulets running off, but there was an eager gleam in his eyes, in the way he scampered along, more stable on four feet than Martin on two. But for all he was a good tracker there wasn't much fight in him, though he bared his teeth and growled willingly enough when the stoat was back up against a corner of rocks. In other circumstances, Martin thought, as he shoved Dog aside and took aim, he'd enjoy the beauty of the little beast. For they *were* beautiful, in their way—the long sinuous bodies, the sharp little faces—and they moved like a dream, not like the poor waddling kakapo, who had at best pace a bastard mix of shuffle and scuttle.

The gun echoed over the island. "Got you," said Martin. "I've fucking got you." The small sleek body was warm in his hands, still. He thought he might try skinning it, not that it had a coat like a possum's but it might be useful someday, and it would be something to do of an evening. He stroked it, admiring, and a little sad as well. A brave little thing, but he couldn't be truly sorry.

He went out again the next day, used Dog's trained nose to track down eight of the kakapo, found the other five the day after that. They blinked at him when he found them, all of them hale enough, and it left him weak in the knees that he'd not let them down, that they hadn't been left a ragged pile of feathers with a broken body beneath.

"No, I'll not leave you," he said, stroking one of the big soft heads. "Don't worry, I'm not going anywhere." They were as good as quarantine, were kakapo. It was as if Resolution had a wall around it of feathers and expectation, a thin wall and a flexible one but one that kept him in regardless. And there was nowhere else for him to be, really. His biology had been ecology and conservation more than anything, his university experience a series of field trips punctuated by lectures, and if there was anyone left out there looking for a cure for plague he'd be pretty bloody useless. Better to stay with the birds and hope that Resolution was isolated enough to keep him healthy, hope that if he caught sick anyway the species barrier would protect them.

They were still, he thought, the more precious population.

"It's a funny thing, yeah?" he said to Dog. "We've been trying to keep those fluffy little bastards alive for so long. For *years*." There'd been a time when the population was less than a hundred, and DOC had an almighty battle pulling them back from the brink. "Now there might just be more of them than there are of us."

It was almost a cheerful thought, though it never lasted. Kakapo were still wavering on the edge—several hundred only, and slow at the breeding—but the establishment of predator-free islands like Codfish and Little Barrier kept them safe from ferrets, from cats and rats and other introduced species that spread over the southern lands like a plague. Resolution was the newest of the refugia, but it wasn't too far off the mainland and rats could float over to it occasionally still, if the tides were right.

The days were a round. Trap, hunt, fish, and the routine of it, the purpose, kept him from feeling alone even though he was.

Then the radio went off, and he was reminded. "Would you listen to that, mate," he said to Dog, a wondering hand resting on the back of Dog's head. "We're not alone after all."

Scientists, more of them, coming in from field work even more remote than his. Isolated, like he was, while the plague burned itself out.

"I'm out on Resolution Island," he said. "With the kakapo." He couldn't leave them.

Turned out, they didn't expect him to. The voice on the radio was almost broken with relief. "They're alive?" it said. "I mean, we sent someone to Codfish, most of them seem alright, we got there quick enough." Little Barrier had fallen. "I know it seems stupid to worry about birds, but, well . . . ."

They weren't about to throw everything over because of apocalypse either. "Seems a bit much, doesn't it?" said the voice. "Better things to do than fight, am I right?" There were plans to retrieve the New Zealanders working at Scott Base, down in the Antarctic. "Some of the penguin guys are shifting over to kakapo." It wasn't as if penguins needed the help. Millions of the bloody things. "We'll get someone over to spell you soon as we can."

"I'm good," said Martin. "I want to stay. Wouldn't say no to some more supplies, though. Pretty sick of fish."

They were setting up in Dunedin, the rest, over on the other side of mainland. "I belong on Resolution," he said. "Me and Dog and the kakapo." Because they'd weathered an apocalypse with him, even if they were too thick to know it, and he wasn't interested in leaving them behind.

"I suppose it's not the first one they've seen off," he said afterwards, to Dog, as they made their way back out into the bush. Their world had ended once, too.

The kakapo that were left, they were the survivors.

Octavia Cade is a New Zealand writer. Her stories have appeared in *Clarkesworld*, *Asimov's*, and *Shimmer*, amongst others. She attended Clarion West 2016 and loves post-apocalyptic stories and science. One of her bucket list goals is to see a live kakapo (at time of writing there were only 148 left, but their numbers are slowly rising).

The Blackthorn Door

Tania Fordwalker

Akari saw the restricted tree first.

Wrestling the Agency's sleek sedan around the treacherous holes in Zimmerman's pitted rural driveway held my full attention. We'd passed the mailbox fifteen minutes back, leaving me certain we'd missed a turnoff to the old man's place—then Akari slapped the dash. "Frank! Pull over!"

Akari snapped off her seatbelt and lunged out the door into the bright summer heat before we stopped moving. Dust and ash-exhaust billowed over the car. My junior agent's silhouette vanished in the rusted cloud. When the air cleared, I saw what she'd seen and fumbled my seatbelt off too.

"Is that a—?"

"*Betula pendula* 'Laciniata'." She stepped aside as I joined her in front of the young tree. "Weeping birch. A Level Four restricted cultivar."

Tendrils of leaves spilled over the pale bent trunk, curtaining it like stringy hair over the face of a cowering girl. I'd only seen this species in file photographs.

My partner puffed out an awed breath. "Just . . . growing out here on the side of the road!"

"I take it he doesn't get many visitors."

Akari took a sample, sealed it in a ziplock baggie. She sat with it smoothed out on her lap as I eased the sedan back onto the dusty road. Would've been nice if the Agency had given us a four-wheel drive for this job, but they'd started phasing them out on account of how much Thaum they burned. Punishing us because the rest of the world couldn't keep their wands in their pants.

None of us had known how hard it would be to find Zimmerman. He was just another name on a shipment list. A wrist to slap. These sorts usually turned out to be crackpots meddling in Low Magic—nutters who thought they could achieve miracles with a stick of willow.

That tree, though? We were here to investigate a shipment of wood, not living trees. That tree had come from a cutting, and it must've been growing here for years. It spoke to forethought. I ran my thumb over the stinging-hot vinyl steering wheel. The office didn't expect us to check in for another six days, and we'd left mobile reception behind forty minutes back. Still, maybe we'd have some news for them earlier than expected.

Akari must have been thinking along the same lines. "D'you think we're onto something?"

"Maybe. One tree does not a thaumaturgical terrorist make."

"Terrorist!" She laughed. "That's a bit racist, Frank."

I bristled. One tree may not make him a terrorist, but Vrata Zimmerman's scant background information, his hectares of bushland in the middle of nowhere, and his name on a list of purchasers of restricted woods sure might. "Call it what you like—I call it sensible caution. He could've slipped into the country with the Thaum refugees—"

"—who've mostly integrated without any issues."

We'd had this argument before. The new agents were all like this, fresh out of university packed to the gills with compulsory diversity units and doublethink. It wasn't their fault—they hadn't even been born back when the Thaum War ended and the flood of refugees began. They didn't know what it had been like. "Tell that to the Fed Square victims."

The kids remembered *that* all right. Akari looked away. "Turn the aircon down, will you?"

My long-sleeved business shirt clung damp to my back after our little botanical excursion. The old scar on my wrist pricked with sweat. "Put on your jacket."

"Environmental vandal."

My fingers tightened on the steering wheel, and then I caught Akari's sidelong grin. It deflated my temper like a pin to a balloon, same as ever. "Latte-sipping tree-hugger."

"Misanthropic dinosaur."

The kid was all right. I never had any of my own—burned through a couple of wives, but no kids. You could do a lot worse than someone like Shoji Akari. She just had to remember to stick to her timbers, and let me handle the arseholes growing them.

We almost missed Zimmerman's place. Tucked away in a grove of eucalypts, the low-slung jumble of timber extensions sprawled in every direction like an aboveground rabbit warren.

We crunched into the yard and parked beside an ancient boxy truck, its tray bristling with shards of eucalyptus bark. Ah, the trusty old inert eucalyptus. If our antipodean woods have any special properties, nobody's been able to tease them out yet. They call Australia a thaumaturgical desert. There's nothing here worth warring over—a curse that became a blessing when the Old Country forests burned. We don't have Thaum, but we've got green trees of the ordinary kind, and blue skies, and clean air. And now every bastard wants a piece of us because half the world incinerated the forests of their enemies into ash but us, well, we're only cooking *slowly*. The lucky country.

The sedan's engine ticked. Akari and I stepped into the oven of late afternoon. I pulled on my jacket despite the heat. Patted my breast pocket to check for my badge, an old habit. Nothing broke the stillness of the place but the shrill of cicadas and the thump of Akari's car door.

She stared at the house, a faint crease shadowing her smooth brow. "This place doesn't look up to code."

"No kidding." I frowned at the tops of trees visible over the back of the low-slung house. I knew the hulk of a willow tree when I saw one.

In the cleared area in front of the house, a charred and blackened circle of ground indicated a recent fire. Ashy scraps of paper twitched in the hot sluggish breeze.

"Look at these timbers!" Akari bounced towards the house. "The window frames on that extension there—look at the colour, the grain. Is that yew? Where the hell did he get yew? Oh my god, and I think this door is golden ash . . . "

Waving her quiet, I knocked on the honeyed wood. I fancied a shimmer of power tingled through my knuckles. Akari brushed a smudge of dust from her dark suit jacket.

The door opened wide. An old man peered out, hunched and tangled as a stunted willow. Watery mud-puddle eyes glimmered over small spectacles curtained between a tangle of grey hair and an unkempt long moustache in the Old Country style. He gave us a grandfatherly smile. Maybe it was the smell of fresh-cut wood that surrounded him, but for the first time in years I thought of Geppetto, the old carpenter from that kids cartoon that got banned after the War.

Akari relaxed beside me. I couldn't blame her. This guy wasn't a danger to anything but sugar cookies.

I flipped open my badge. "Mr Zimmerman? I'm Senior Agent Francis Sawyer, and this is Probationary Agent Shoji Akari of the Thaumaturgical Regulatory Agency, Division of Restricted Materials. We'd like to ask you a few questions concerning a shipment of timber you received in late November last year."

The old man's smile brightened. "Oh! I've been expecting you." His accent was pure Old Country, as though he spoke with a large marble cupped on his tongue. "Please, come in. Come. I have ginger beer." He turned from the door and shuffled back into the cool dim of the house before I could respond. A keyring at the belt of his trousers jingled like a cat collar in the gloom. I pocketed my badge and followed him into the narrow hall at a polite half-speed, casting a glance back at Akari.

Expecting us? she mouthed.

Most of the doors in the hall were shut, bar two at the end: a cramped kitchen and the stuffy, windowless sitting room Zimmerman deposited us in before he left to fetch drinks.

If something was amiss in the house, it wasn't in this stark room. The elderly have what Akari would call a 'gendered' divide when it comes to mess. If there's a woman involved, you'll see doilies and pointless little china figures. You'll smell polish. And once you're sitting down, good luck getting up again through all the cushions and rugs and crap strewn around the place. Houses like those are clean but cluttered. This sitting room told me that Zimmerman had no woman in his life. The wooden furnishings were sturdy and finely made, but nothing adorned their surfaces except a layer of dust. In the far corner, a hutch held a white rabbit splayed out in a nest of straw, asleep, breathing in that rapid way rabbits do.

Akari and I perched on the edge of a settee with wooden arms carved to resemble ocean waves, as beautiful as the pea-green upholstery was ugly. I touched the timber waves. Perhaps this was the ultimate fate of that shipment of blackthorn. I glanced at Akari to confirm. She shook her head.

"He takes his doors seriously though," she murmured. This room had two: the heavy hallway door we'd entered through, and what must have been the back door, a sliding screen made of some kind of translucent paper over a light lattice of wood, diffusing green daylight into the dingy room. Akari inclined her head to the open hallway door. "Notice anything weird?"

I frowned at it. "Frame's reinforced with metal."

"Oh," she said. "I meant the doorknob. It doesn't have one. Just a deadbolt on the other side."

A little spasm of suspicion shot down my spine.

Akari nudged me and pointed at the other door. "It's fine. He's no Buffalo Bill, and that sliding door is practically plywood and tissue paper. You could huff and puff your way out of here, Frank."

"I knew you kept me around for something."

"It's your sunny personality."

Zimmerman shuffled back into the room, clutching two chipped mugs. He pressed these into our hands and eased himself down into the worn armchair with a sigh.

"Now," he said at last, "best we talk."

"It's the blackthorn, Mr Zimmerman. Your name appears on a shipping regist—" The hall door slammed shut. I sloshed ginger beer onto my shirtsleeve. Beside me, Akari laughed, hand splayed across her heart.

Only Zimmerman seemed unfazed. "Again it does this! Perhaps this house has ghosts. When you are old, always you live with ghosts."

Biting back annoyance, I rubbed at my wet sleeve, only half-aware of the rough circle of scar tissue under the thin cotton.

"Or, perhaps I have hung the door wrong." Zimmerman got to his feet. "The frame is solid though. That is the important—ah!" He'd reached for the keys at his waist, but they weren't there.

That little crease reappeared between Akari's straight black brows as she studied the sturdy facade of the closed door. "Are we locked in?"

"No, no. We can get out through the back door." He sat back down and gave Akari a sad smile. "My memory these days is not so good. You know how it is, when you walk through a door and forget what it was you meant to get."

I let go of my wrist and splayed my fingers, fighting the urge to make a fist as my adrenalin ebbed. "Why the security, Mr Zimmerman? Are you expecting trouble?"

Zimmerman said, with utmost seriousness, "I do not like

doorknobs."

Christ. We were stuck with a batty old bloke from the Old Country who bought in a bit of illegal wood because that's how things were back in his day. At his age he wouldn't even get time, he'd only waste a lot of ours.

I cleared my throat. "To the matter of the wood . . . ."

"It has a name, this effect."

"Pardon?"

"The forgetting, made by doors. This is the 'event boundary'."

"We need to talk about the wood."

"Yes." His voice hinted impatience. "I bought it. And many more such shipments before."

Akari and I exchanged a glance.

"Whatever I could find, I tried," Zimmerman continued, waving a knobbled and unconcerned hand. "But blackthorn is best for my purposes, you see."

Akari put her drink aside and leaned forward. "And what are your purposes, Mr Zimmerman?"

"Forgetting. As I have said."

"You were building . . . doors?"

"Let me start from the beginning," said Zimmerman. "Let me start from the war."

I suppressed a sigh. Sure, let's go back thirty-five years and listen to this senile old man's life story. We TRA agents had nothing better to do with your tax dollars.

Ever the good cop to my bad one, Akari fished a notepad from her jacket pocket and studied the old man, pen poised to strike.

"In the Old Country, I was a carpenter." He paused, his eyes moving from Akari's face to mine. "I know what you are thinking. I was not part of the development of large-scale thaumaturgy, and I wanted no part in it. A brute goes first to force, and misses finesse. You see. This energy in the woods, it can bring light, and it can bring warmth, but the Steuernden sought only to bring fire. I lived on the coast with my family and used Low Magic to make furniture, seeking always to learn what shape the woods wished to become, and what gifts were locked in these forms.

"When we began to lose the war—when the United Forces bombed the Schwarzwald-Projekt base and killed most of the High Thaumagi—the Steuernden soon came looking for everyone else who worked wood. They were not asking."

I pressed my lips together and raised my empty mug to my face to hide my expression. There's not a Thaumagus alive who doesn't squeal about how pure and innocent they were during the war. The rapt attention on Akari's face made her seem childlike. It left me with a twinge of something like exasperation, something like affection. I bet she was one of those kids who brought home any half-dead wild animal she found and then cried when the thing bit her.

"My wife died early in the war," said Zimmerman. "Always she was ill, and soon the food and hospital bed shortages—well. It was only my daughter and I left when I heard the Steuernden were sending troops. So we ran, all the way to the other side of the world. I gave my life savings to a man with a ship and we came across the ocean, and your border patrols picked us up and put us in a refugee camp. For three years we—"

"Mr Zimmerman, with all due respect, we're here to talk about a shipment of another sort," I said. The air around Akari turned frosty, though to her credit she barely twitched. My left hand clenched in a stranglehold around my right wrist, flesh and bone tight across the numbness of the two crescent scars. "The government has the utmost sympathy for your situation as a refugee, but legal reparation was made decades ago, and that's not—"

"My daughter," Zimmerman interrupted, "died two nights after our resettlement on the mainland. I found her hanging from the doorknob in her bedroom."

His words hung in the air. I'd seen a couple of short drops in my time at the camps. Nasty way to go.

Akari's hands twisted in her lap. "I'm sorry."

"So am I," said the old man. "Pain such as this takes root in your mind. It can never be unmade. Would that I could open a door and step back to the time before I fled the Old Country, I would let the Steuernden take me." He looked me in the eye. "If it saved my daughter, Agent Sawyer, I would set fire to the world."

Twenty years with the TRA, and that was the first time a suspect ever said something like that to my face. "Tell me about the doors, Mr Zimmerman."

"The doors. Yes. I had reason to think of doors, after what happened. I dreamed of them, many times. So, when the reparation money came, I bought this land, and started building my house, and I began to make doors. I made doors of golden ash and silver birch, doors of willow, bloodwood and yew . . . ."

Beside me, Akari bit her lip and made a few reluctant notes.

"Some thaumaturgical woods worked better than others. Certain dimensions helped also. To test my doors, I wrote a number of items in a list, then stepped through the door, and wrote again as many items as I remembered on the other side. The doors were working, but not enough: I would forget minutes, even an hour, but I could not forget my pain. So still, I worked.

"I learned soon that the active part was not the door, but the frame, saving me much time. I found later that I could layer the doors, pressing many frames together in a row, allowing me to combine different woods. Advancement was slow; the materials were costly and hard to get—you know this well. The risk made me economical, made me experiment with thinner layers of door-frame. This necessity led to my finest breakthrough: making the frames thinner did not make them less powerful, so I could stack many more into a smaller space. A day came when I walked through a doorway made of more than sixty thin frames. I forgot the past week of my life.

"When the forgetting grew bad enough to be inconvenient," he said, "I started writing a letter to my daughter each time I was to test the door. I pinned it to my shirt before I stepped, so I could read it after, and remind myself what I was doing, and why. It felt like talking with her."

I tried to catch Akari's eye, wondering if she could shed any light on what sounded like the ravings of a lunatic. I'd never heard of thaumaturgy used like this before. Parlour tricks, yes. City-levelling explosions, absolutely. But if the old man was telling the truth, he'd created something else altogether. Something subtle and dangerous.

"You don't believe me," he said. Astute.

"It's quite a story."

"Here." With a grunt, he pushed himself up from the arm-chair and hobbled to the rabbit hutch in the corner. As he unlatched it, I swallowed back a surge of unease.

Zimmerman lifted the rabbit out of the cage and carried it to the coffee table. I thought for a moment that the limp, motion-less creature must be dead. I hadn't seen it move once during

Zimmerman's tale. But when he lay it on its side on the table I saw again the rapid rise and fall of its chest, the black shining stare of its open eye.

"What's wrong with it?" Akari's voice was uncharacteristically flat.

"You know." Zimmerman fixed her with those still pondwater eyes. "It's been through the door. Washed clean. Even the motor skills, vanished. All it has now is reflex . . . to suckle, to breathe—and it can feel sensation, though I cannot say if it knows what is pleasure and what is pain. When the body passes through the door the mind is left behind."

I touched the rabbit's soft fur, waved a hand above the open eye. Nothing. "How does it work?"

"Truly, I cannot say. It is like a magnet to a computer disk. Or like a fire to a shrub. It does something to the mind. Takes the tangled pathways you've grown in your head over the years and burns them away." Zimmerman gathered the limp rabbit in his puckered hands.

"It's cruel," Akari said.

I made a mental note to talk to my junior agent about emotional overinvestment when all this was over.

"Life is cruel, young lady. This creature is at peace." The old man walked to the hutch but seemed reluctant to let the rabbit go. His bony hand smoothed, smoothed the long white ears. He lingered, half turned away in the corner of the room where the shadows gathered. "I put them down humanely after the tests. This one, I kept alive to show you."

He'd implied knowledge of our arrival before, too. "What made you so sure we were coming?"

"I've been buying restricted wood for thirty years, and never have I been on a watch list until now. Why do you think this is?"

"You wanted the TRA to come."

"You're very close to the truth of it, Agent Sawyer."

I wondered if it was as simple as him needing his story heard. Or perhaps after thirty years of work he realised he could sell his door; profit might satisfy him more than artificially induced dementia. Hell, maybe when he'd finally faced the reality of wiping himself out of existence, he just chickened out.

I remembered the burned papers out front and realised I

wasn't wondering—I was hoping. Some thought scratched at the back of my mind like small fingernails clawing at me and I couldn't let it through, not yet. Not that memory.

Zimmerman spoke again, almost too low to hear. "As the door grew stronger a strange thing happened—I no longer wanted to forget. You see, her death had begun to recede into the past over time, but the door washed away those years, day by day. The past—her death—crept back towards me, and so did my rage. Forgetting her wasn't enough. I had to avenge her."

"Avenge her? How?" Akari's voice tremored.

"It's already done."

Akari jolted to her feet. I put my hand on her arm and moved her behind me. She stumbled on the coffee table, clung to my wrist. Not for the first time, I wished they gave us TRA agents sidearms, or even truncheons. My hand itched to close around a truncheon again. All that had stopped after the fuss over the refugee camps.

Zimmerman looked over his shoulder at last, his eyes malevolent, his eyes clear. His eyes so very young. "My daughter was too ashamed to tell her Vati much of what happened to her in the camp, but I knew enough to know when. She was not the same, after. Once the reparation trials released the guard duty rosters, I knew who."

Akari clung to my wrist, her frightened eyes piercing me "Frank? What is this?"

I remembered another pair of frightened eyes. They'd been the colour of pond water. My dry throat clicked. "You've made a mistake. I never knew any Zimmermans."

"Our name was Janus," he said. "Perhaps you don't remember that, but she left you with a reminder, didn't she? My daughter had a crooked front tooth. What is on your wrist, Frank Sawyer?"

I jerked my arm away from Akari, but I knew she'd touched it through my sleeve as she clung to me, felt the two rough crescent scars of the bite I'd never had treated. I saw the terrible knowing in Akari's eyes. I turned away. "Christ. I don't know how it happened. I was young and angry."

"So am I," said the old man. He settled the rabbit against his chest, stroking it with his free hand.

"You can't do this. She hasn't done anything wrong." I reached back for Akari's arm. She recoiled from my touch.

The old man watched us, eyes bright and clear in his seamed face.

"You can't keep us here!" I snarled.

"You are not prisoners, Agent Sawyer. On the contrary, you should not linger. I may have forgotten to turn off the oven. My memory these days is not good." He slid open the flimsy screen door.

With a dull, shocked understanding I knew what the odd thickness of the frame behind it meant. I knew the meaning of the strange texture of the wood, the fine ridges pressed together dense as the grooves on a record. Thousands upon thousands of sliver-thin frames. Beyond the doorway, sunset filtered through narrow bars of bone-white birch.

The old man turned away from us, cradling the rabbit on his shoulder like a sleeping child. "You are free to leave whenever you please," he said, and stepped out into the light.

Tania Fordwalker lives two lives. In one, she's an illustrator and art director for tabletop games. In another, she writes speculative short stories and YA novels. The thread that binds her varied work together is the desire to make people feel something. Working from her home studio in Tasmania's mysterious far south, Tania loves hiking, cider, good movies, bad movies, and building a real corker of a fire in the wood stove. You can find her work online at www.TaniaWalker.com.

The Eater of Dirt

Marie Vibbert

Among her many names, the one that remains is Eater of Dirt. The rest have been cast off, but one name is enough to sustain her. The filth-goddess knows the flavor of fairy footsteps, the crumble of dead magic and the taste of tiny living jewels with wings that crunch in her teeth. Men may fling her holy name about as an insult, but they don't know how sweet and savory and fulsome on the tongue dirt can be.

She was once a goddess of purification and lust with stone temples and glistening priestesses in cloaks painstakingly sewn of feathers and beetles. Young men gazed at the walls that encircled her rites and yearned for the barest syllable of knowledge to pass from those red-stained mouths to theirs. Any one of those boys would leap to her pleasure, and did, and she tasted their youth and fears when she grew bored with supping on the death of trees, of monsters, of orchids.

Time grinds temples to gravel. Fires wash trees to ash. There are no more fairies and monsters to dine on. She learns the taste of oil-slick and lead. Women forge handles out of words and grasp and sort and judge concepts as they once did weapons or fruit. Humans become too self-aware to worship any being too like themselves. The gods are trimmed: The hands and eyes and scepters cut away, anything that will hold a handle.

The Eater of Dirt persists, minus her earlobes, her feathered headdress, her girdle of insects. So much waste. Long after the Sky and the Warring Twins and the Judge perish, she tastes their trimmed-off attributes in a tea of autumn leaves or a confetti of salt-washed shells.

New gods are forged with vague shapes, wrapped in contradictions and paradoxes to confound the handles. They have the illusion of permanence in their first blush of adolescence.

New cults reap and sew inedible fetishes for their new gods. More than she can digest, and not filling in the slightest. The plastic confetti and weeds of propylene stick in her gums and she despairs.

She squats beside tiny worshipers, sometimes a rabbit,

sometimes an iguana. They bend their knees and open their mouths to the Eater of Dirt. Together they savor histories digested, civilizations mulched.

She will outlast because humans still kneel to her. Still reach soft, plump fingers like worms into her repast and lift it to slick wet tongues.

"No, that's dirt, baby!"

True worship is compulsion, and the compulsion persists, to taste the world. Like the compulsion to attach words, to kill and mourn magic in the same breath.

"Should we call the doctor?"

"She'll be fine. All children eat dirt."

The tiny priestess laughs, her teeth delicately lined in grains of darkness. She revels in the fulsome earth and her prayer is sustaining.

Humanity will forget the goddess, but never forget the banquet: soft and grit, fresh and old. She is in their tongues and teeth and throats and in the urge forever to open, to taste, to savor. And so she will survive, and eat the new gods, returning all to earth when its time comes.

Besides selling thirty-odd short stories (six to *Analog*!), twenty-some poems and a few comics, Marie Vibbert has been a medieval (SCA) squire, ridden 17% of the roller coasters in the United States and has played O-line and D-line for the Cleveland Fusion women's tackle football team. Her college coursework was in Environmental Geology but by day she is a computer programmer.

Under the Sunset Hill

Soumya Sundar Mukherjee

Walking through the forest under the lights of the setting sun, I asked, "Is this all true?"

Pervu said, "Nobody here lies about the Sunset Hill, but the city-people rarely believe what we say, Sir." The way he spoke made it clear that he didn't have much respect for the city-people. An awkward silence fell as we walked, crushing the fallen yellow leaves under our feet.

When I questioned his ability to serve me as a guide, Pervu had admitted he was seventy-three. But he had been walking with me for almost two hours in this hilly forest area without a sign of tiredness. The old man was thin, but his bones had more strength than mine.

The sad light of the afternoon rested on the top of the towering trees. Cold had started to rise from the dark reddish earth. The crickets had already begun to sing. Rabbits crossed our path several times; once I spotted an iguana behind a bush. The forest seemed full of animals.

I noticed a spotted deer through the long Sal trees. It seemed to have no fear of us as we stopped to look closely at its beautiful hide.

None of the animals had run away seeing us. That seemed strange to me.

Pervu had spent his whole life in the forests of the Belpahari region. Breaking the silence, I prompted, "It's good to see so many animals here."

Pervu's eyes narrowed suspiciously. "Why, Sir?"

"Just saying," I said.

His face had suddenly changed color, but he didn't say anything more. I saw that he was lost in thought, walking like a robot along his familiar forest path.

We saw three more deer in the next five minutes.

Pervu warned me, "Not that way, Sir. Follow me; this is one of the shortcuts."

The way he led me was hardly a way. Through the gaps

between the huge trees were only more trees. The sun had leaned more to the west. Flocks of birds were returning to their nests and we could hear their cries overhead.

Suddenly Pervu asked, “Do you like hunting, Sir?” There was something strange in his voice.

“Hunting? No, Pervu. I don’t enjoy taking innocent lives. Why do you ask?”

He must have sensed my curiosity. He said, “It’s a long story. Would you like to hear it?”

“Why not?” I said. “But tell me, first, is this really a shortcut? We’ve been walking for hours. How much further to the ashram, Pervu?”

Pervu said, “Not much. One branch of this shortcut leads directly to the foot of the Sunset Hill. Hundreds of wild beasts roam freely at that part of the forest. That’s why it was once the poachers’ favourite part of the forest. But you know, Sir, now even they don’t want to go there.”

I hazarded a guess at his strange demeanor. “Don’t be afraid if something dangerous happens to cross our path. I have a revolver with me.”

Pervu said, “I know. It’s under your shirt, left side. Am I correct, Sir?”

I was so astonished that for a moment I couldn’t speak.

He said, “You don’t like hunting; then why are you carrying the gun with you, Sir? Don’t you want a rabbit, or at least a wild turkey?”

I recovered with a smile. “I’m a policeman, Pervu. Carrying the service revolver has become a habit even when I’m just out travelling. And I’m not interested in your rabbit or wild turkey, thank you very much. Now please walk faster, and take me to the ashram through your favourite shortcut before it’s too dark in here.”

Pervu smiled and again I had that uncomfortable feeling. *Is the old man hiding something from me?*

Our path was gradually becoming more prominent. It was evident that Pervu knew this jungle’s alleys well. He said, “Let me tell you the story then, it will help to pass the time.”

A hyena saw us coming and sat down to watch us. The sun moved behind the pillars of the trees.

Pervu met Sardar Harman Singh in this very forest. The forest was younger then; so was Pervu. The mighty Sunset Hill loomed at the northern end of the forest, as it had from the beginning of time. Sardarji beckoned him with his fingers. The fingers held a five hundred rupee note.

Pervu had never touched a five hundred note in his lifetime. He felt an urge to hold it in his own hands. His family was so poor that they used to eat ant-eggs at dinner. Pervu's little sister was an expert at robbing those delicacies from the ant-holes.

Sardarji said, "This is yours, boy, if you do as I say."

Pervu's eyes brightened. "What do you want me to do?"

"I need you to go with me to the forest under that hill. Tonight."

Pervu retreated at once. Everybody knew that that part of the forest was not to be visited even in the broad daylight. *And here's this man, speaking of going there at night!* No amount of money could make him say 'yes'. "I'm sorry, Sardarji."

Sardarji's gigantic figure advanced upon him. When the boot hit his abdomen, Pervu was so surprised at first he felt no pain, only the strange feeling of flying through the air. The pain came when he landed upon the dried leaves.

"Bastard!" Sardarji bellowed. "Nobody survives saying 'no' to Sardar Harman Singh, you dirty beggar."

Shivering in pain and fear, Pervu saw the unshaking muzzle of a revolver pointed at his chest. He tried to remember his little sister's face for the last time.

Then the muzzle dropped. Sardarji said, "Well, you get to live this time, boy, because I need you." The five hundred note was replaced by a thousand rupee note. "What do you say now, beggar boy?"

The face of his sister flashed before Pervu's eyes again. *This note could change our lives.* But that part of the forest was forbidden after sunset!

Sardarji said, "Let me put it straight for you, boy. Either you take the money and walk with me, or I shoot a hole in your worthless skull and walk alone. I give you thirty seconds. What do you want?"

Pervu said what he had to. "I'm going with you."

"Good," Sardarji said. "Now pick up that box and start moving."

Pervu wanted to run, for he knew that what they were about to do was not only forbidden but wrong. He knew why Sardarji wanted to go to the foot of the Sunset Hill. He tried for the last time. "Sardarji, that place is not good at night."

Sardarji laughed. "I know, I know. I've heard the story of that f***ing Keeper."

Pervu shivered, hearing the name of the Lord, the Keeper of the Forest, uttered with so much irreverence. He silently prayed, "Forgive me, O Lord! I've said nothing bad about you!"

He said again, "Sardarji, those who have gone there to hunt, have never . . . ."

"Returned?" Sardarji snarled and showed him the revolver again. "If I don't return, you will rot there with me."

Pervu lifted the large box Sardarji had with him. He didn't need to open it to know what was inside.

The Keeper of the Forest wouldn't be happy! *Forgive me, Lord.*

Pervu wanted to cry. If he didn't return, his parents would never be able to find a suitor for his beloved sister, for he was the only earning member of the family.

He recalled a saying he had heard from his father, who had taught him to look for the signs the forest gave to those who knew to see them. His eyes fixed upon a Neem tree that was gradually darkening under the twilight.

"One sparrow—no fear.

Two sparrows—dead tear."

He remembered his father's voice and prayed with his whole heart for the sight of one sparrow flying away from that tree.

Two sparrows flew from the tree's leafy crown.

As they approached the part of the forest beneath the Sunset Hill, Sardarji said, "I know there are rare black bucks in this forest. Do you know how much money that animal may earn you, you beggar?"

Pervu said nothing.

"More than you can imagine. So open that box and help me fix the gun."

They fitted the parts of the rifle together in silence. Finally Sardarji adjusted the scope and said, "Let's go."

They came to a juncture where the narrow road went into three different ways. They took the one that went north, and after fifteen more minutes' walk, came almost under the Sunset Hill in the light of the sunset. To Pervu, it stood like a colossal, dark prohibition. In front of that enormity, Sardarji seemed even less significant that an ant.

Sardarji ordered him to stop at the edge of a rainwater pond. The tall trees seemed to be getting closer to each other in the spreading darkness. The silent air was almost suffocating. Sardarji climbed a tree and ordered him to climb another. As Pervu adjusted himself on the branches of the Jamun tree, Sardarji got ready with the rifle, facing the pond.

The black buck appeared at once.

Pervu remembered another lesson his father had taught him. *The animals we see in the forest might not be just what we see.*

Sardarji aimed his rifle; the black buck was drinking water at the edge of the pond. Pervu almost forgot to breathe.

He heard the sound of the gun. He was taken aback discovering the buck standing upright beside the pond just as before.

Sardarji has missed!

It was unbelievable. Such little distance and such a steady hand, yet the animal was calmly walking back into the forest, clearly not afraid.

Even Sardarji himself couldn't believe his own eyes. "How did I miss that f***ing beast?" he murmured. He climbed down from the tree and ordered Pervu to come down, too. "Come on. I'm not going to spare it."

Sardarji started following the buck. Pervu knew that this was his chance to run away, but he didn't. A strange attraction lured him behind Sardarji to the Hill. He thought he knew what waited at the end of this drama, but it was as if the Hill wanted him to witness the 'how'.

Another gunshot, another miss. The long muzzle gave off an

uneven trail of smoke.

The black buck waited unaffected a few metres away, as if tempting him to try again.

Sardarji wiped perspiration from his forehead. "What the hell is happening? This time I'm sure I hit it!"

Pervu said, "I told you not to come here, Sardarji. There's still time; let's go back, please."

"You shut up, beggar's son! You got the money; now do as I tell you."

Sardarji reloaded the rifle. The black buck retreated through the jungle at the foot of the hill. Once, it turned its head, as if to see whether they were still following.

Pervu knew that black bucks couldn't smile. *It must be an illusion!*

The buck ran, and they ran behind it. They ran until they came to the very foot of the great Sunset Hill.

The buck waited for them under a big Shimul tree. Sardarji uttered under his breath, "This time you'll taste real hotness, my friend!"

But Pervu noticed another thing under the tree. An old, rusty rifle, half-buried in the ground. Must be the property of a hunter who never returned. He remembered the scene of the two sparrows flying away from the tree. He was breathing hard. His heart was pounding dangerously just under his throat.

Sardarji's gun thundered again.

"Got him!" Sardarji punched the air in excitement.

The black buck was lying on the ground. Sardarji proudly moved to his prey. The forest looked denser than ever in the darkness. Silence prevailed; even the crickets were not singing.

Suddenly Pervu felt that he was sinking in the hard ground, as if he had been standing on quicksand. The earth was swallowing him.

Panic-stricken, he screamed, "Sardarji!"

Sardarji ignored his cry; he was gazing at the buck on the ground.

The black buck was not dead yet. Its legs were still trembling a little. But, Pervu sensed, something more was happening around them.

The earth had captured him; he wasn't sinking anymore, but

he couldn't move, only watch, and he realised this was his role: *to see.*

The black buck was transforming. Its hind legs became the paws of a lion; its teeth changed to the fangs of wild dogs, its front legs to human hands and its body to a human torso. Its eyes shone like two burning stars. The figure stood up.

"Oh, Lord!" Pervu whispered.

The rifle dropped from Sardarji's hand; he stood petrified in front of that terrifying presence. The whole forest was filled with the unearthly red glow radiating from the furious entity. It seemed that the trees were on fire.

Two jackals passed Pervu and went to the place where Sardarji had been standing. Pervu saw hundreds of animals gathering round them to see the final moments of the man who had come to kill them. The red glow made them all red—their fur, their fangs, their paws, their eyes all warmed with the angry hue. They stood motionless, as if they, too, didn't belong to the realm of the living.

The eyes of the entity were burning like coal, and Sardarji's eyes were fixed on those glowing fireballs. His mouth was open, his hands were stiff. It came forward and touched Sardarji's forehead with a burning finger.

Pervu lost consciousness with the explosion. In his dream he saw the dust from Sardarji's disintegrated body getting mixed with the forest soil.

When he came back to his senses, he found himself lying at the familiar juncture of the three paths, although he couldn't make out how he had come to this place. But he could recognize the Neem tree from which the two sparrows flew away.

He would have dismissed the whole incident as a dream, but the thousand rupee note inside his shirt-pocket was more than real.

We were still walking on the forest path when Pervu finished his story. He said, "Not only Sardarji, but a lot of poachers tasted that same medicine. No poacher returns after visiting that place."

Pervu had the gift of making an unbelievable story palatable.

I was about to tell him just that when, all of a sudden, he fell to my feet and started crying.

"Hey! Hey! What are you doing, old man?" I was so surprised that for a moment I didn't know what to do.

I helped him to his feet. Tears were still pouring out of his eyes.

"What is it, Pervu?" I asked. "Why on earth are you crying like this?"

"Forgive me, Sir." He was still unable to speak properly. His body was convulsing with powerful emotion. "Forgive me. I misjudged you."

I was more astonished than ever. "What the hell are you talking about? What misjudgement?"

Pervu grabbed my hand and said, "Forgive me, Sir. You talked about the animals in the forest, and I saw your hidden revolver. I thought that you, too, had come to kill them."

A bit harshly I asked, "What made you realise your mistake, wise man?"

Pervu pointed his fingers to a tree. "Look there."

I at once saw the black buck looking at me from behind the tree. I couldn't understand what Pervu meant.

I was going to say something when I noticed the beast's eyes. They were glowing *like two burning stars.*

Pervu again fell at my feet. "I've lured you with my story under the Sunset Hill. This is no shortcut, Sir. I thought that if you'd come to poach, He'd take care of you."

I couldn't decide how angry I should be with him. The black buck was calmly watching us.

"But the Lord, the Keeper of the Forest, has shown me that you're a good man, Sir," Pervu said again. "Please forgive me, Sir. Please."

Black bucks can't smile. I know that black bucks don't smile. And their eyes don't shine like stars. It must be an illusion!

The buck moved away from us, deeper into the forest. The enormous presence of the Sunset Hill hulked behind the darkening trees.

My voice trembled when I spoke. "How do you know that I'm a good man, Pervu?"

"The Keeper of the Forest knows everything of nature; human

nature, too. There! Look there!"

From the branches of a tall Neem tree, a little sparrow flew away.

Pervu whispered, "One sparrow—no fear. Let's go back, Sir."

Soumya Sundar Mukherjee is an admirer of engaging speculative fiction. A bi-lingual writer from West Bengal, India, he writes about stuff strange dreams are made of. His works have appeared in *Mother of Invention Anthology, Occult Detective Quarterly*, *Hidden Animals Anthology* and a number of other places. He spends his leisure time in writing, studying the myths and legends of different cultures around the globe and drawing monsters both horrifying and cute.

The World Ended in Ice

Adam Stemple

The world ended in ice
as scientists predicted
lab coat Noahs
ignored
as they counted the animals
two by two
into their ark
and lifted off

We who are left
shiver
in the cold
in the dark
in our ignorance and greed
forgotten sinners
with no dove
to fly from Ararat

Adam Stemple (www.adamstemple.com) is an author, poet, musician, web designer, artist, and professional card player.

Exit Here

Andrew Kozma

It was the year the lake turned to glass. It was as though the water wasn't even there, the shore simply extending further and further into a barren landscape. The lakes had been cleaned in recent years, some meager effort to beautify the city, but that made it all the worse. Every discarded bottle, every useless tire rolled into the surf, they petulantly stared back at you when you walked along the water. It wasn't just the trash, either. The lake itself turned malevolent.

I was part of the team trying to figure out how to save the lake. Or maybe what had happened to it. Or, more specific to my actual job description, how to get the public to accept the lake as it now was—as a blessing rather than a curse, a sign of the times which no one wanted to read, but everyone already knew said EXIT HERE.

We had a set-up on the unpopulated side of the lake in an area which had been poisoned long ago by a paper mill but the city swore wasn't toxic anymore. Nobody believed the city, not even those of us who worked for them. It wasn't just that the grassy slopes of the hills around us looked like mange, patches of dry dirt resistant to grass, the soil powdery to the touch. The air had an oily feel. It settled in the lungs like a conscience. And the animals. I had trouble looking at them, even the malformed rabbit Talia took in and designated the project pet. Talia was a biologist, but not a very good one. To be honest, none of us were very good at our jobs, which is why we had *this* job. City finances being what they were, people left if they had any other option, and only came for work when the rest of the world failed to appreciate their virtues.

And, to be fair, the rabbit fit right in. It had one eye permanently half-closed, while the other eye's pupil was blown out. Its teeth were too short and its limbs were too long and seemingly all different sizes, so it moved with an awkward hop where it was never quite clear what direction it was heading. Talia had named the rabbit Thumper.

We lived and worked in a concrete warehouse. It had been built as a boathouse right before the lake began to die in earnest and had never been used. But instead of being fresh and new, a few years of abandonment had rubbed the concrete raw, smooth and discolored. Pink. Concrete shouldn't be pink, should it? Like skin trying its damnedest to heal? But we made the best of our new home. Yiannis, the chemist, hung tarps as tapestries and painted them with correction fluid and agar, abstracted images of the landscape and the lake. His hills were filled with mold. The bottom of the lake seeped rust.

Out at the lake's edge, I took pictures. This was more time-consuming than it should have been, since the water only shone at the right angle, and if the lake wasn't visible, then how could I convince people the lake was worth saving?

Klarissa followed behind me as I snapped pictures, deliberately scrunching her feet through the crackling, pristine sand. The sand had been imported years before, back when the city was a tourist destination. Enough sand to bury a small town.

"It's beautiful, isn't it?" she said.

"It's water."

"Still. Despite that. Just look at it. Could you paint something as perfect?"

"No."

We all had little quirks, strangenesses we had to get used to in hope the others would endure ours. Klarissa was simply blind to the world, seeing everything as separate from her. As if life was a casual stroll through a museum and one day you died lonely and forgotten in a niche the docents hadn't even been to in years, surrounded by minor Renaissance still lifes.

But she was right. The lake looked like a painting by someone who couldn't paint anything living, and so just cut animals and people out of the equation entirely. The water glowed. The sky was feathered with clouds. Far in the distance was an island with a few brown sticks of trees which looked like telephone poles waiting for harvest. And closer by, a yacht rested on the lake floor without any obvious damage. The red hull was as lurid as a fresh scab.

Klarissa was an urban planning specialist; her job focused on how to get the water to be drinkable, sustainable, and unpollutable. Inside our warehouse, she flashprinted miniature dioramas of her plans, all of the pipes and water pumps and filtration systems working at that tiny scale. It didn't matter how much she planned, though, if the lake refused to live again.

We had a time limit. The city wouldn't tell us what the time limit was, but we were instructed to hurry. Lack of sleep was encouraged, as was generous use of the stimulant provided to us. The time limit was tied into the vegetation death encroaching on the city's shores. That was one thing. Another was the diminishing population. Not through death. Well, not that we were told, anyway. Houses were being abandoned at an alarming rate. Put up for sale and then evacuated. Eviscerated. Every last appliance. Every built-in shelf. As if the owners knew the house was never going to sell and they were never coming back.

Harold was the project leader and also a philosopher. Not just in temperament, but in occupation. He'd headed a philosophy program at a sub-Ivy League East Coast school before being driven out by some scandal he refused to discuss and I refused to look up. Not out of respect for privacy, but for fear of what I'd find. It was easier to live not knowing.

"We can't live in ignorance!" Harold said at almost every weekly meeting. "What happened to the lake is our fault, and we can only atone for what we've done when we've fully admitted what we've done."

"This isn't a religion, Harry," Yiannis said. Talia nodded, petting Thumper.

"Isn't it?" Harold pressed.

I expected Nadia, our geneticist, to argue with him, but she refused to look up from the table. Her hands were splayed on the surface like she was going to push herself up and away from this entire conversation, this entire place. But her fingers only twitched impotently.

She hadn't realized before arriving that all of this was our fault. Or, more specifically, her fault. The fault of geneticists like her who believed in the power of their newly strengthened science. The Yellowgills invaded the lake due to people dumping the troublesome, custom-engineered pets they no longer wanted into the freshwater because they didn't want to kill them; eventually the Yellowgill population grew so thick schools of them were chopped up by powerboats, so the geneticists created Razortooth Gar. The Razortooth Gar decimated the Yellowgills, as well as every other fish in the lake. A disease named Red Rot was introduced to the Razortooth Gar and ruined their gills so they suffocated, which resulted in a thick scum of dead fish on the lake's surface. Worse, the disease bacteria mutated so it separated from the fish entirely and turned the lake maroon, clouding the water and staining the flesh of anyone who swam in the lake. And so modified Gullet Mussels were seeded to filter the water clean. That last was a success. They filtered the lake clean of everything.

We each did our jobs, such as they were. Harold took everything we did and combined it into reports, which he sent off to the city. He never told us the results of those reports, just patted us on the back whenever he saw us, smiling beneath his thin moustache in a way that was meant to be comforting but always came off as the smile a priest gives a person about to be executed.

It sounds dark. It was dark. Even during the clear, fine days of spring and in the height of summer, sunlight skipped over us. It shunted off to the city itself, that distant line of buildings that glittered in the light like frosting on a cake in a display window. None of us had been back there since our jobs began. Regularly, automated ferries crossed the lake bringing supplies. We were cut off.

But there was still beauty to be had. Playing with Thumper. Walking through Yiannis' garden, laying bets on what each seed would look like after growing up through the poisoned soil. Celebrating each newly launched experiment of Nadia's, drinking champagne as the spider-legged frog skittered into the water or a jar full of net-winged insects twirled and dove over the surface, chitinous bodies already crisping in the lake's vaporous glare. Sitting at the end of the long dock, staring down through the water to the perfectly clear lake floor, imagining it as a long drop through the air, as though I were on a cliff rather than just a few feet away from what would hold me up, what wouldn't let me sink.

We made no progress. The land refused us. Nadia's various animals, slowly or quickly, all died. The chemical composition of the lake and the soil fluctuated, but from poison to poison. My record of events was one of failure, and no one read it. Maybe after the city was dead, the city and all its surroundings a shell, someone would come and find the diary of our efforts and understand the obvious thing that eluded us.

"We can't give up," Klarissa told me. She'd caught me at the end of the dock dangling my camera over the water's edge.

"I'm not giving up. I'm admitting defeat." I firmed my grip

on the camera strap, but still held it over the water. "Let's just go somewhere else. Somewhere living."

She nodded across at the city. "They're counting on us."

"You don't care about them."

It was true. Her voice was flat. It was just a talking point, what we were supposed to repeat in our heads when depression came calling. But what I was feeling wasn't depression, but elation. Excitement. To leave. To get the hell out of that hell.

"Maybe." She wouldn't admit it. It was hard, I knew, because that's what I'd been wrestling with for weeks. "But there's no point in running, because there's nowhere to run. What happened here, we'll take it with us. The poison is in us."

I argued. I tried to convince her to come with me to the coast, that we could start a new life, the city and the lake and everything here be damned. The lake didn't want us here. Nothing wanted us here. Everything we'd tried, I rehashed it right then and demolished every one of her objections, but she didn't budge.

"I don't need to convince you," I said finally, pissed off, and threw the camera into the lake, except Klarissa caught the strap.

"No."

I was done with words. I yanked the camera back, but she wouldn't let go. The dock rocked beneath us, and we didn't care. We grunted and pulled and pushed. She was stronger than me, and she tugged so hard I fell into her. We tumbled onto the sun-worn wood, the camera between us. It broke with a snap, and we stopped struggling.

Klarissa rolled off me and sat up, pointedly looking away from me, out at the lake and the city's ghostly skyline. "You got what you wanted."

The body of the camera looked undamaged, but the lens had shattered, lacerating my fingers. The cuts were shallow but bled freely. Exhausted emotionally, physically, mentally, I stretched out on the dock, head and arms over the side, and lowered the camera into the water. None of this was what I wanted.

The dock shuddered as Klarissa rose to her feet and walked back toward the warehouse. Blood from my cuts dripped into the water, each drop spreading like cream into coffee. The breezeless air settled around me like a second skin.

I didn't realize it at first, but my blood was changing something in the water. The red didn't just spread out and disappear, it drifted away in fractal swirls, as though something was sucking it up. Where my blood dripped, the water turned from glass into, well, simply water.

"Klarissa!" I called out, and she ran back at the excitement in my voice. Seconds later, she was stretched out next to me, watching my blood slowly drip with the same fascination. She was there when the silt below us popped with a dozen tiny cloudbursts and the most miniscule fish I'd ever seen swam up to us, so transparent they were just bones with peppercorns for eyes.

I unstrapped my utility knife from my belt and flicked the blade open. The first cut was hard to do, a thick jag across the meat of my thumb, but the others came easier. I wasn't killing myself. I didn't want to die. But the pain, oh, it felt good, if only because with every slurry of my blood into the lake, more happened in the water, the blood setting an entire cascade of consequences into action. It was hypnotizing. I only heard the tail end of Klarissa calling the others on her phone, saying they needed to come down to the dock quick.

Then she held out her hand for the knife.

"My turn."

Andrew Kozma's fiction has been published in *Escape Pod*, *Mythic*, *Daily Science Fiction*, and *Interzone*. His book of poems, *City of Regret* (Zone 3 Press, 2007), won the Zone 3 First Book Award.

Portrait by Wolf William Say.

Vivian, Radiant

Bernadette Marie Oliver

Uncle Jessie crushed Vivian into the snow. The coldness seeped under the flaps of her hunting jacket—at her wrists where her gloves didn't meet her sleeves, at her back as her shirt rode up over her belt. Blood trickled over her lips from the cut left by Jessie's pinky ring. Her vision was murky under his clouded breath.

She flailed, wrenched an arm free from Jessie's grasp, and frantically felt around until she found the pulleys of her compound bow. She ripped the bow from the snow and smashed it against Jessie's head, and he collapsed.

She got to her feet as fast as she could. The tree line was about ninety feet from her. The trees would provide cover if Jessie pulled his .45. Vivian could make it to the trees, just like stealing second base.

Will sat hump in the pickup, sandwiched between her dad and Rick, a fellow sales rep. Her left leg crooked away from the gearshift and Dad's belly pressed against her right side. Even with the stark, white mountains and the blue vaulted sky, the trip here had been uncomfortable at best. First, her dad had only spoken a few words to her the whole flight out from Philly. And then there was Dad's business partner "Uncle" Jessie, and his son, and the nephew. Will was sure Jessie knew about her. But Dad never did anything about Uncle Jessie's teasing. Like a brother, Dad called him. Will saw him more as Dad's master.

Every November, Will put on her best butch one leg at a time. She read the newspaper's sports page the week before they made the trek from Philly to Uncle Jessie's ranch outside of Coeur D'Alene. She cut her hair short and tight. She packed flannel shirts, duck canvas overpants from Orvis, and her Barbour winter hunting jacket. The jacket was one of the benefits of guilting Dad about how she was a good son on these business trips, that this should be a business expense, and since it was a business trip she should look professional.

When she got the jacket, her sister, Peg, said, "Big whoop, it's a jacket," and she said, "But it's a Barbour hunting jacket. Now I look like Papa Hemingway," and her sister said, "What? You gonna draw the beard on?" And she would practice her hunting walk—slow movements, careful not to stumble, one move every thirty breaths. She was skilled at developing camouflage.

All the way up, Dad and Rick talked about work. They talked about crossbow sales versus compound sales versus recurve sales. They talked about the 1994 "Get Your Kid Outdoors" campaign.

"Where you going to high school next year?" Rick asked.

"Saint Joe's."

"Third generation McAddams," Dad beamed.

"Playing ball there?"

"Dunno."

"He'll try out." Dad gently shouldered Will.

She winced as a cascading sharpness traveled down her spine. "Yeah. I guess." Her camouflage was fading.

"Will had the highest batting average this past season," Dad said. Her Dad put as much effort into butching her up as she did.

"Really," said Rick. "What was your average, Will?"

"625." She squirmed a bit at being praised for hitting a ball with a bat.

"625?" Rick paused for patronizing effect. "That's phenomenal. You have another Babe Ruth on your hands here, Mike."

"I know. I know," Dad boasted. "It was like every time he was up, you knew he was going to crack that bat. Now if I could only get him interested in golf."

"Golf's boring, Dad."

"You better not let Jessie hear you say that," Rick quipped. "You'll break his heart."

"As long as you play something. Maybe you can get a scholarship to college for playing ball. God knows how I'm going to afford it."

Will closed her eyes and prayed for college to come soon and end these trips.

Ahead, the wire and wood-post gate, adorned with a red and white caution triangle, emerged from the soft snowdrifts.

At night, Will would float up the Wissahickon River, along the bluffs. Among the twisted curtains of wisteria, Novo, the Eastern Elk, the last of his kind, would wait for her. She'd throw her arms around his neck, bury her face in his reddish coat. She'd feel the softness of his fur, smell soil and lilacs, and hear distant rain. They'd travel into the deep, dark woods, Novo's antlers glowing silver in the moonlight. They'd move through brambles past warm, shiny houses dotting the borders of the Wissahickon Valley. Peering in the windows, watching people moving inside, Novo would say, "Time will come. You will be the person you are to be. I will be there."

Will hoped if she prayed long enough, at some point she'd wake up and be correct. Be the daughter her mom wanted. Be able to show her dad who she really was and say to him, "See. God did make me this way."

Her sister Peg never had a problem with her being who she was, though she didn't see the point in becoming a woman.

"You've never had a period. It's not something to envy, in fact it can be cruel sometimes."

"It means you get to have a child."

"If you want kids, you can meet a nice guy and adopt mine. God knows I don't want them."

"I may not want to be with a guy."

"Wait, so you're a lesbian?"

"It's about who I am."

"Big words for the little man."

"I'm not a man." She turned away from Peg.

Peg sidled up to her and said, "Whatever you want to be is okay with me, but stop being such a girl about it."

Will's head sank. Her chin plowed into her chest. Peg lifted her face in her hands.

"I'm kidding, Will. You'll always be my little sister."

Uncle Jessie told his son Travis and his nephew Kyle that they were old enough to do the fire themselves. Will sat still, tucked away in the overstuffed wingback chair in the far corner, reading Uncle Jessie's copy of *The Archer's Bible*. Hiding in a tree waiting for the bears to pass.

Travis and Kyle poked at the newspaper ash under the logs, making sparks jump. They added more newspaper, but the fire didn't take hold.

"Fer Chrissakes, you pansies, can't you even start a fire," said Uncle Jessie.

Kyle rolled his eyes. "I dunno. Maybe, the logs are wet. You do it."

Uncle Jessie bellowed, "I told you to do it."

Travis flinched. "We're trying."

"You sound like your fucking mother, Travis." Uncle Jessie grabbed another beer from the refrigerator. He leaned the bottle cap on the counter and slammed his palm down on the bottle. "Ow. Fuck." Uncle Jessie shook his hand in the air. Kyle and Travis guffawed.

"The bottle opener is on the counter right there, retard," said Will's Dad.

"Some help you are, Mike. You could have told me before."

"Looked like you had it under control."

"When does he have anything under control?" asked Rick.

Uncle Jessie grabbed his crotch. "Bite this, smart ass. Where's that fire, boys? Hey, Will, what you doing? You staring like a queer or something? Go help those numb nuts."

Will's tree was shaken. She smacked her book closed, hoping her father would dissuade Jessie from making her come down. But Dad said, "You heard the man, son. Help those two get a fire going."

"We don't need his help, we can do it. He doesn't know how to start a fire," said Travis.

"Where is it then?" asked Uncle Jessie.

Will sauntered across the room, making sure to show that this was no big deal, as if she was always fixing the numb nuts' messes. If she stopped, she would be shaking. If she tripped, she would cry.

She paid attention to the folds in the threadbare Persian rug.

When she got close, Travis said, "Nice John Wayne, Willy."

She repressed a wince. Will guessed that if she started giving orders, the boys would follow. She reached into the woodpile and pulled out a wedge of birch with peeling bark. She handed it to Kyle. "Get your knife and peel this."

"Who the hell do you think you are?"

"We need kindling." She grabbed a fire tong, pulled the pieces from the fireplace and placed them in front of Travis. "Split these. They're too big."

Uncle Jessie barked, "You heard the man. Get going, boys."

She separated out twigs and small branches from the half-cord and stacked them as a triangle in the middle of the ash pile. She shredded newspaper, mixed that with the bark shavings, and gently placed them in the triangle. She took one of the pieces Travis had split, placed it in the iron cradle and lit the pile underneath. The wood caught fire, and she added more. Setting the fire would be her task for the rest of the trip, which wouldn't be so bad. She could focus on this and not have to deal with them.

Travis knelt down next to her and whispered, "Willy, you know what they call bundles of wood used to start fires? Faggots."

When Will was five, her mom took her to the Academy of Natural Sciences to see a dinosaur exhibit. In the end it wasn't the giant Tyrannosaurus skeleton or the dino dioramas that interested her, but a small exhibit about recently extinct animals. She became fixated on one animal, the Eastern Elk. It used to range all over Pennsylvania. And it had been alive when her great, great grandfather was alive. That was only two greats, so it wasn't that long ago. Also, it was huge, one thousand pounds, and its antlers were six feet across. The exhibit didn't have any skeletons, but they had a cartoon of the large reddish elk standing next to a picture of a white-tailed deer for comparison. Her mom said that the last one was killed a long time ago. Why would we want to kill them all? Mom didn't know. Underneath the picture was the word Novo. Mom said that was its name. Novo the Elk. Maybe if Will prayed enough, Novo would come back, she'd see him in the forest, and they'd be friends.

When Will was four, Peg would play dress-up with her. Parade her around in their mother's clothing and high heels.

Mom would tell Dad, "It's normal. Just a way for him to play with his big sis."

But occasionally, Mom would see her in a dress with a string of costume jewelry, and she could tell that Mom saw her as a girl. Except for the short hair, Mom and Will looked so much alike in pictures— tall, thin, with delicate features.

When she was six, she and Peg were in the same ballet class, but Will was the better dancer. She'd flit and float about the room, lifting the girls into the air. Her mom was proud of her at recital— one of only four other boys.

Mom would tell Dad, "He's good. Maybe he'll be the next Baryshnikov."

When she was eight, Peg and Will would play ballet Barbies in the foyer for hours.

Mom would tell Dad, "Some boys play with dolls. He'll be a nurturer. Maybe a doctor, or a therapist, or something."

When Will was eight and a half, Mom asked, "What do you want to be when you grow up?"

"I want to grow up and be a beautiful prima ballerina."

That was when Mom made it all stop. Dance lessons, over. Baseball. No touching the dresses. Slacks and Oxford shirts. The dolls donated to Goodwill. Will got balls and bats instead. Mom schooled her in performance. Don't cross your legs. Relax. You don't have to look like you're at attention. Don't shake someone's hand like that. Let me show you. Don't do that. That, don't!

Each change became a sticky, stinging layer of new, uncomfortable skin. But in her room Will had secret stashes. When she was alone she would lock the door and retrieve makeup and bits of clothing from secret spaces. She'd dress herself out, paint herself into existence.

Up ahead of Vivian, the thicket gave way to a grove, and beyond the grove was a clearing. The flat sky was turning a darker, metallic gray. Maybe an hour more of daylight. If she could get back to the snowmobiles, maybe someone would be there, then Jessie wouldn't touch her. The worst thing that could happen was that Dad would blame her for ruining the trip. But then she wouldn't have to come back.

Despite Rick's size, Will was thankful when she'd get paired up with Rick. He didn't want much of anything from Will but to be quiet when needed. The frigid air and snowy forest made it easy to be silent.

The tree stand was crowded with the two of them.

"Did you say something, Will?"

"No."

"It doesn't matter. Nothing's been by. I think we got a stinker spot today." Rick paused. "How's school?"

"Good, I guess." Rick talking with her wasn't part of their script. She wondered how she would get down.

"Will, I want to tell you something. I watch you try and stay out of sight. You don't try to mix with us, which is perfectly fine."

Throwing herself out of the tree stand seemed a good option. It was only fifteen feet to the bottom.

"But you know," continued Rick, "a couple years off, when you get to college, do whatever the hell you want. Do whatever makes you happy."

"Okay." Will shifted in her seat, moving toward the ladder.

"No, listen. I say this because, while you're a good partner up here, sitting so still, I can tell you don't want to be here. That's okay. When I was a young kid, I didn't look forward to my father's hunting trips, either. It wasn't until I was older that I appreciated it and took it up again. I'm not saying that's what you have to do.

I'm just saying that for a while I didn't do this. Couldn't even think of sitting in a tree stand for hours on end waiting for some deer to wander by. Part of that was because I didn't want to do it anymore, but most of it was because my father made me. Ya get me?"

Will nodded.

"And choose a college far from your parents. Somewhere you can find out who you are without them, ya know. Somewhere your friends become family. I did that at least. But most importantly, do what you want to do when you get there. You want to do theater, you act your ass off. You want to major in English, write a fucking book. You want to do music, out-compose Mozart. Do what you want. Do who you want. Don't listen to us. The world changes as you grow older, and the things you did to please your parents don't really matter. They just make you neurotic. Don't listen to us old men. We haven't a fucking clue. We're all posing at being the men our fathers wanted us to be, and it ain't cracked up for shit. The secret is, if you're happy, your parents will, most likely, be happy. And if not, fuck 'em."

Rick made Will feel uncomfortable, but also instantaneously became the coolest man she knew.

Will curled up on Novo's back as they climbed up the mountain. The wind whipped stinging shards of ice and snow at them, but with Novo's breath, the snow and ice turned to gold and silver dust and glittered through the air. At the top of the mountain, through the blizzard, Will could see the Winter Palace. The bright red crest of the palace crowned through the silvery clouds. The light from the gate cut a path through the storm, showing them the way. As they ascended, Will could hear a choir of children singing. The choral voices soared over the din of the wind and rang out, "Be not afraid. Change is at hand."

The gas station attendant didn't look like he belonged out here in Idaho or Washington, wherever they were. His hair was long. He wore a black leather jacket, a royal blue gas station uniform shirt with the collar popped, and a bright shiny red scarf. His fingernails were painted a lush, deep purple. Small chrome hoop earrings dangled from each ear. Will, hiding in the candy aisle, couldn't help but gawk at him. Here was this gas station boy out in the middle of nowhere, where it was dangerous to be someone like them, at least according to what Peg told her. Before she went on these trips Peg would tell her stories of boys and girls beaten to death for being queer, for being different. She told her of Brandon Teena. But here was this boy in a gas station where lots of people saw him.

Gas Station Boy's lips were thin and probably cold. With a nice shade of pink to compliment the scarf, a bit of pencil, and some lip gloss to finish, Will could make his lips seem fuller, softer, warmer.

Kyle shoved Will into the Charleston Chews. "Wake up."

Travis cackled. "It's past his beddy-bye."

"Hey, Willy, check this out." Kyle reached under his jacket and pulled out a copy of Penthouse opened to a scene where a girl was kneeling in front of a guy, his gooey, gloppy emission all over her face.

Will averted her gaze.

"He totally spooged on her. And she loved it. You like spooge, Willy?" Travis said.

"Hey," the Gas Station Boy shouted. "Put the porn down."

Kyle ripped at Will's jacket and stuffed the magazine down her collar. "He's the one doing it." Cackling, Travis and Kyle ran out the door, leaving Will with Gas Station Boy and a dirty magazine in her jacket.

"You going to pay for that?"

Will walked up to Gas Station Boy, placed the crumpled Penthouse on the counter, and tried to smooth it out. The edges were stubborn. She tried to smile. "I got to go."

As she stepped away, Gas Station Boy grabbed her wrist. With the world crashing inside of her, all Will could do was manage a squeaky, "Please."

Will had lots of friends at four, five, six, seven and even when she was eight. But after eight was nine, and by then she knew all the ways she was different. She would try and talk with other kids, but it was like they could tell she was this mannequin wearing the right clothes, walking, talking, standing, sitting in the right ways. For her tenth birthday, Mom asked her to start making the list of people she wanted to invite to her party, but the last two people she was on regular speaking terms with, Jenny and Gabby, had moved up the social ladder and stopped talking to her. Will wasn't even on the social ladder. That was when she thought of the zoo.

And that was what they'd done every birthday for the past four years. Mom didn't want to deal with the extra kids and Will didn't want to let Mom know that there weren't any kids to deal with. The zoo was her, Mom, and sometimes Peg. Dad would figure out something else to do.

At the zoo, most animals were grouped, and isolated, according to their differences. Some were allowed to be together, like chickens and goats in the petting zoo, or birds in the aviary, though they were still all birds. And the monkeys and apes were all sad and despondent. They'd shuffle around their enclosure, then when they remembered that they were a monkey they'd burst across, swinging from ropes, and screech at the people staring. One moment still and distant, then angry, wanting to shout, "This is not who I am! This is not where I belong! Look at me!"

At the zoo, people watched the animals and not her. No one really looked at each other.

On her twelfth birthday, she noticed a chimp in the far corner of the chimpanzee enclosure. The other chimps were hanging out together, and this one was huddled in the corner banging its head against a wall, over and over, each time with greater force. Then, with one particularly hard whack that made a small resound in the enclosure, the chimp stopped. No one noticed what had happened. People were moving on. Mom stood by the exit and beckoned. She looked back at the chimp, and on its forehead was a spot of blood, and in its eyes a distance so secret, so familiar.

That night Mom made homemade mac and cheese, and

tomato soup. Dad asked, "How was the zoo?"

Will explained the event with the chimp and asked, knowing the answer, "Why do you think she did that?"

Dad said, "It's sick or something."

Peg said, "Probably had a fight with her parents."

Mom said, "I don't think that happened."

"I saw it."

"You only think you saw that. Monkeys don't get like that, they're animals."

"I was there and I saw that happen."

"I was there too and I didn't see it. You are misremembering it."

"Why? Why do you think that?" asked Will.

"Because if I saw that I would have said something to someone and you are only bringing it up now," said Mom.

Dad asked, "Is there cake tonight?"

Later, she went back to her room, took out her cutting kit, laid out her supplies, freed the blade from the plastic, and went to that old, secret, familiar place.

She tried to hide her glances at the satin pearl gown with the delicate bead trim and the matching heels. She stood at a blouse rack shuffling shirts, catching glimpses of it between each hanger. It beamed moonlight. When Peg walked up to her and whispered, "It's too expensive," she wasn't that surprised her sister had noticed. They were at the store for Peg's homecoming dress, for a homecoming she didn't even want to go to. She said it really wasn't that big a deal, and she didn't have a date. Mom had convinced her to get some of her friends to go stag.

"It's your senior year and it'll be one of those things you'll remember for the rest of your life," Mom said.

"You said that of my perm in fourth grade."

"You still remember it."

Will pleaded with her sister repeatedly to go, but Peg avoided answering or said no. But then one day after school, Peg said, "It's all worked out. I'm going, little sis. But you have to promise to go to the pre-dance event with me."

So a deal was struck. Will would go to the pre-dance event and be social. Peg would go to the dance and afterward give her the dress.

Their mom stood with an armful of dresses, each one more ruffled and garish than the last.

Will was mortified when Peg asked, "Can't I get a suit?" But admittedly every party dress was a pooper. "Then find me a dress, Coco."

"We're looking for *a* dress. It doesn't have to be a *party* dress." And off she went into the business suit section and found a casual romper-style dress, with a black felt finish and a Madeline collar. She paired it with red tights. Definitely Peg. "You can wear your Doc Martins with this and it'd still look cute."

Their mom was happy they found something, even though it wasn't what she would have chosen.

Vivian's heart was pounding, deafening. She couldn't hear Uncle Jessie, but it didn't matter. The swath of snow, grass, and branches she'd left behind her gave him a clear path to follow. In the clearing, footprints plodded down a slight slope, surrounded by a tunnel of denuded aspen. Only a few more steps to home base. Someone would be there; it was almost time to go home.

As they passed through the gates of the Winter Palace and entered the courtyard, Will felt a rapid, growing wave deep in her chest. Around the courtyard stood people with smooth skin and gentle features, people who were neither young or old, male nor female. People of many colors all dressed in gowns of moonlight. Novo knelt, and Will climbed off his back.

Novo nuzzled her hand and spoke. "You are home, beloved. Do not be afraid. I will be with you."

And out of the heavens appeared a blinding brilliance, bathing Novo and Will. A thousand feathers brushed against her skin, and when they dissipated, only Will was left. And she shone with the brilliance of ten thousand moons.

On every hunting trip Will would plan out her movements before they all settled into the cabin. The fact that everyone was habitual made things easy. Last year had been different. Last year she screwed up.

The schedule was the same. The boys all were sent to bed before ten and the men would stay up another hour or so. If the men were really drunk, everyone retired at the same time. At the beginning of each trip Travis had trouble sleeping and was up and down all night. Uncle Jessie was the first awake, sometime around three. Will's dad pooped after coffee around five, and he was in the bathroom for at least twenty minutes, sometimes thirty. There was only one bathroom, which was disgusting, but the door closed and locked.

Will determined that she had between twelve and two in the morning to do what she had to. Last year, she'd overslept the last night of the trip, waking up just before two. She grabbed her kit from where it was stashed behind the headboard and crept through the cabin, fast, but quiet. It was never safe, but she needed the release. All trip Uncle Jessie had called her a pussy, or a fag, or a fairy, because Will still didn't want to learn how to field dress the deer. Her dad was disappointed, because his shoulders rose each time Uncle Jessie said it. Dad would tell Jessie that Will wasn't ready yet, maybe next year. That was the extent of the defense.

Will folded her pajama pants neatly and placed them on the sink counter. She opened her kit, laying out her cutting pieces. She pressed the tip of the blade into her left calf. A small cut and the bite from the alcohol was enough tonight. The pain first, then the wash of bliss as the inside trickled out. Then someone knocked on the door.

"I'll be done in a second."

Will panicked. She threw everything in her kit, grabbed a wad of toilet paper and pressed it against her wound. She grabbed another handful of tissue and wet it under the faucet to wipe down the blood on the floor and tub. When she turned back to shut off the faucet, she knocked her pj pants into the sink. They were soaked.

"Come on, Will. I got to shit," said Uncle Jessie.

She forgot that she was wearing her pink briefs. She had begged Mom for pink underwear when she was eight and they were boy's underwear. She still tried to fit into them, though they were faded, becoming threadbare, the elastic wearing out. She was so careful to keep these things hidden about herself. She took care. She planned. She gathered her things. She shut off the light. She unlocked the door. There stood Uncle Jessie.

"You take longer than my wife." Uncle Jessie turned on the light. "What happened to you?"

"I got my pants wet."

"Did you piss yourself?"

"No. I. It was in here."

Uncle Jessie closed his hand in a loose circle and moved it up and down in the air. "Were you jerking off?" he whispered.

"No."

"Are those pink underwear?" Uncle Jessie grabbed Will's shoulder and pressed her against the door frame. "You shouldn't wear those around here." He leaned down and said in a low, grumbling wheeze, "Someone may mistake you for a girl, and you wouldn't want that."

Uncle Jessie's heavy hand pushed against her shoulder. Will heard footsteps in the living room and Jessie looked away. Will slithered out from his grasp and headed down the hallway.

"Nice ass, Sally."

This year, she hadn't snuck off to cut herself. She watched Jessie watch her. Her dad never mentioned anything to her, so Jessie must never have told him. Will kept her distance and tried to avoid being alone with him.

Peg pulled up to a large, colonial-style house. There were several other cars in the driveway and high schoolers milling about outside, smoking.

"I thought we were going to school for the pre-event," asked Will.

"Stop it, nosy. Be patient," said Peg. "We're here."

"This is the homecoming pre-event?"

She touched Will's shoulder. "Don't worry. It'll be fun."

The house was teeming with people. On the stairs, two boys were kissing. In the living room, girls were slow-dancing together. Will tugged her tie.

Peg took her hand and squeezed it. "Don't be worried. These are our people." She called out, "Claire. Claire."

A tall woman pushed through the hallway full of partiers. With her red stilettos, she towered over the both of them. Her hair was long, jet black, with blunt, straight bangs. Her long gown and lipstick matched her heels. She had a sparkly black choker around her neck with matching earrings and bracelet. She was beautiful.

"Hi, Peg. Who is the starlet with you?"

"This is Will."

"I've heard so much about you," Claire said.

"Is it ready?" asked Peg.

"Of course. I have four Boy Scout badges for preparedness. Are *you* ready, Will?"

"Ready for what?"

"It's a surprise," said Peg.

Claire led them upstairs past the kissing boys, past the people with mohawks, past kids sitting on the floor waiting for the bathroom, and into a large bedroom. Across the bedroom, hanging on the wardrobe, was the satin pearl gown with the matching shoes.

"What did you do, Peg?" asked Will.

"Claire works at the store and she got me a discount. I used my money from working at the deli this summer, and with the discount it was enough."

"I can't do this. What about Mom and Dad?"

"Fuck 'em. They're not here. Besides, I really want to see my little sister."

Claire handed Will the gown. "Hon, it's not about the clothes. It's how you feel inside. But if you want to wear this dress, you have to lose the school picture suit."

They sent Will into the en suite bathroom. She took off her clothes and slipped into the gown. In the mirror she looked like a boy in a dress. At the store, she'd pictured herself magically turning into her real self. She wanted to hide, to rip off her dead skin. She wanted to scream. Peg heard her, came in and hugged her.

Claire stood at the door. "Don't be sad, starlet. We're not done yet."

"What happened to your arms, Will?" Peg pointed at the marks on her inner arms.

Claire interrupted, "Not to worry. Okay, Peg?" She led Peg away to the door. "Let's bring your sister into the world. Wait out here."

After Peg was outside, Claire motioned to the vanity and told Will, "Have a seat."

The vanity was right out of some famous theatre, with wigs and makeup displayed for an actress preparing for a big role. But the role Will had prepared for was being Will.

"What's your real name? Do you know it?"

Will had always known her name. Though she'd never met her grandmother, it was her name, too. "Vivian."

"Vivian? That's a fantastic name. What color is your hair, Vivian?"

Will chose a short, bobbed, blonde wig. Peg's hair was short and blonde. They'd look like sisters now.

She began to pin Will's hair back. "It's a brave thing you are doing. I know being yourself, your true self, can be dangerous."

Claire fitted the wig onto Will's head. Though the change was small, for the first time since she was little, she could almost see herself.

"But you need to stay brave. Other people depend on that brave heart. But most of all, Vivian, you must be brave for you." Claire touched Will's chest, but then moved her hand to the inside of Will's arm. She traced a scar, a scar Will had made when she was ten. One of the first.

"The world doesn't need another dead girl. We need a bright, shining light; your light. You've got to fight for yourself, Vivian. That means recognizing who you are, even when everyone else wants you to forget. I know that fear and loneliness seem endless, but you have to reach out, find help, find others like us."

She spun Will around, then dipped a small applicator into a concealer cream and began to apply it. "You're lucky. You're not alone. Your sister loves you. I had five brothers, no sisters. I would have liked one of them to be as loving and supportive as Peg. I have my Aunt Theresa, though, which is lucky for me because she let me move in here after high school. She's helped me with becoming the woman I am."

"And that's what Peg is doing?"

"Right. When I was starting, Aunt Theresa told me to do this—when someone puts you down for being the girl you are, say 'I am she. I am Vivian.' Try it."

"I am she. I am Vivian," said Will.

"That's a good first go, but ya got to reach deep down inside."

Will thought back to when she'd never worried about he or she, to the time when she was Vivian, to a time when she didn't have to be reminded. Dancing was where she found herself. Dancing in ballet class, twirling and whirling, pirouettes and pliés.

"I am she. I am Vivian." Her voice bounced off the ceiling.

"Whenever you need strength, remember who you are, and say that."

Claire finished with a light pink lip gloss. "Vivian, you have a long, wonderful future ahead of you. Difficult maybe, but wonderful." She turned the chair around and in the mirror was Vivian, radiant. She looked so much like Mom. She started to tremble.

"Oh, honey. Why don't we call your big sis in, okay?"

Claire pulled Vivian behind her and called to Peg. Peg opened the door and came into the room and tried to peek behind Claire. "Hold on, you're going to ruin the reveal. Peg, I present your sister, Vivian."

This was who she'd always been. She knew Peg could see that, because Peg couldn't stop crying. She knew Peg could feel that, because Peg had never held her that close before.

But with each mile home, Will reappeared layer by layer and Vivian disappeared bit by bit. Peg said they could sneak in, and Will could stay Vivian for a while more. But they should have left Vivian at the party.

Their parents were waiting on the couch.

"Take that off," Dad said so loud the windows rattled.

Peg tried to explain while Will pulled out the bobby pins. Mom pleaded with Dad not to be so hard on "him."

Dad ripped the wig from her head. "It's not coming off fast enough."

"Stop, Mike. Stop."

"Listen, Will. You can't embarrass your mother and me by doing this shit while you're under our roof. You want to make a fucking fool of yourself when you are older? Fine. You're on your own then. But while you are here, Goddamnit, you will follow our rules."

At five they assembled in the living area. Will dreaded this every morning, but especially this morning. She'd been paired up with Dad and Rick for most of the week, and the previous night Uncle Jessie had smacked her on the shoulder and said, "We gonna get ourselves a deer tomorrow, dude?" It was his turn.

Outside, Rick raced off into the black on his snowmobile with Kyle chasing after. Their headlights lit up the mountainside with each dip and dart, each drift and ditch.

Dad walked up to her, gently placed his hand on Will's back, and asked more than stated, "You guys will be okay."

"We're going to be great, Mike. Don't you worry, we'll come back with two bucks," said Uncle Jessie.

Will turned the key on her snowmobile and heard a series of clicks.

"Damn boy, whatcha do?" shouted Uncle Jessie.

"Way to go, Will," said Travis. "Now we're going to miss everything."

"I didn't do anything."

Jessie and Dad started inspecting the vehicle. Gas in the tank, lights turned on, battery okay.

Dad said, "Throw your kit on mine and ride with me."

"He can ride with me," said Jessie. "I don't mind."

"No offense, Jessie, but you'd never make it up the trail with the two of you on your sled."

Travis snickered and Uncle Jessie shot him a scowl.

She put her gear on top of her dad's and tied it down. Jessie and Travis took off. She climbed on behind her dad and held onto the rails.

"Put your arms around me. It'll be safer."

Will seldom ever hugged her father. She moved her arms around her dad's waist. "You can hold on tighter than that. I won't break." As they went into the mountains, Will squeezed her dad. The snow glittered in the headlights.

At the top of the trail, over her dad's shoulder, the massive silhouette of Uncle Jessie stood waiting. She was hoping that Jessie had left with Travis.

"Get your stuff, Will. Let's go. We're burning daylight," said Uncle Jessie.

She grabbed her pack, quiver and bow.

"We'll see you back here in the afternoon," said Dad.

"I'll take care of him, Mike." Jessie turned and headed down the trail lined with bare aspen to the clearing. Will made sure to hang back some, enough to keep him at a safe distance, but trying not to seem bothersome. They traipsed down the trail through the snow. Her dad stood at the top framed by the tunnel of trees, his face lit by the first rays of sunlight.

Will didn't recognize where they were headed. Jessie had spotted a small group of deer, and they stalked them the first thing out. Will kept mental notes of things they passed—a grove, a stand of trees, a small mountain creek—in case they couldn't find their way back.

They broke for a lunch: nuts, water, and jerky. Jessie produced a flask from under his jacket and took a swig.

"We'll get close enough to them. It's a matter of time."

In the clear cold air, the sharp alcohol smell stung her nose. "Yeah. Okay."

Jessie put the flask away, and the black-checkered handle of a .45 peeked out from inside his snow pants. "Why don't you take the lead this time? You ever stalk?" asked Uncle Jessie.

"Not really."

"Well, you're going to do it today."

Will soon picked up the trail again. The snow was matted

down from their hoofprints, but she couldn't really tell the direction. She guessed they were headed up the mountainside, where there was less cover and they could see who might be coming for them. Will tried to pick up the pace and maintain her physical separation from Jessie. She could hear Jessie panting as they headed higher.

The sun was getting shallow in the sky, and the shadows of the trees were getting longer along the snowbanks. Will spotted the herd, dotting the landscape like little marzipan deer on icing. She blindly waved at Uncle Jessie to stop, but kept hearing the crunching of snow. She turned back and Jessie loomed over her.

"Will."

"What is it?"

Jessie punched her square in the mouth and Will hit the ground.

"You're teasing me and it's got to stop."

Will's world was wobbly and watery.

"I know you want to," Jessie panted.

She tried to push off the ground, but Jessie descended on her, suffocating her. Color started to drain from the sky, and her vision filled with a swarm of static. Jessie clawed at her jacket and she tried to push him away.

If she died, no one would miss her. Maybe Peg. Peg would. But her Mom and Dad would probably be relieved. They would welcome not having to worry about her embarrassing them. They wouldn't need to explain her to family or friends. Dad could go on these hunting trips all the time if he wanted. Will had no friends, she had done nothing with her life yet. Maybe this was what was supposed to happen to her. Maybe it was better to let it happen.

"Will."

Jessie's shadow moved, and sunlight warmed her face. Then she remembered what Novo had said: she was not who she was to be, yet. She remembered her name, and remembered that brief moment when she could see Vivian's future ahead of her.

"I am she."

Vivian reached out for her bow.

No one was at the rendezvous point. Vivian was winded and weak. She clambered around the snowmobiles looking for keys, but none were there. She heard a rustling in a clump of evergreen bushes a few yards from where she stood. She took an arrow from her quiver, strung it in front of the release loop, clicked in her trigger to the loop, and pulled back the bowstring. Her arms trembled. She tried to line up the peep sight with the twenty-yard pin, but she couldn't get the pin centered. She only had one shot before he'd get off a round.

The bush moved and she let the arrow fly. A piercing wail of pain sounded, and a young bull elk crashed through the thicket. The arrow had landed squarely in his neck, almost invisible except for the orange fletching. The elk bolted into the clearing, stopped and locked eyes with Vivian. Clumps of snow spotted his forehead and muzzle. He blinked, and flakes fell from his eyes and sparkled in the last bit of sun. The young elk shivered, crumpled, and fell. He lay on the ground, heaving, steam curling from his nose and mouth. The snowy footprints started to turn red where he lay.

She knelt next to him. She could smell the soil, lilac, and the promise of spring rain. She lifted the mounds of red wetness, pressing it against his wound, stuffing the blood back in.

"I didn't mean to. I didn't mean to." Under her hand, his heartbeat slowed. The snow crunched behind her.

"You got one," said Dad. "Look, Travis, Will got an elk! What's that? A six point!"

Will, that name was so distant.

"We've been out all along the ridge and didn't get near anything, and here you are back at camp and there's an elk," said Dad.

"This isn't me. I don't want to do this anymore."

Dad touched Vivian's face. "What happened? Your lip is all busted up."

Vivian buried herself in his chest and sobbed.

"Okay. Okay." He held her tight. "Hey, Jessie, what happened to Will?"

"Nothing. He fell."

Jessie tucked his gun under his belt.

"Why do you have your gun out," asked Dad.

"What does it matter?"

"Did he hit you, Will?"

She nodded.

Jessie said, "Fucking . . . ." and Dad punched him in the jaw. Jessie stumbled, and her dad grabbed his coat and pulled Jessie back into another punch. Jessie threw his arms around him and they crashed to the ground. Dad landed on top and pounded Jessie's head on the ground.

"Travis," Jessie called out.

Travis stuttered a step, then stood still. "Dad, come on."

Dad dropped his guard and shouted, "Stay out of this, Travis."

Jessie punched him in the gut and the face. He pushed her dad off and got to his feet. He drew his gun. Then she heard a whistling overhead, followed by the thwack of an arrow hitting the ground.

Jessie jumped back and swung his barrel toward her. "Fuck, Rick!"

Rick nocked an arrow and drew a bead on Jessie. "You can stop now. It's all over."

"Over, huh? What's over?" shouted Jessie. "You think you can shoot me before I shoot you?"

She heard the whine of a compound pulley, as Kyle aimed at Rick.

"Good boy, Kyle!" Jessie pointed his .45 back at her dad.

"Dad, come on. Stop, please," wailed Travis. He swayed in the snow, hugged himself across his upper chest, eyes squeezed shut.

"Such a fucking disappointment. You're a limp-wristed pussy like Will there," said Jessie.

Travis buried his face in the crook of his arms. Vivian noticed that he was starting to shake.

"You're a fucking weak monster," said Vivian. "Gotta rape a girl out in the woods to feel strong. Huh?"

Jessie huffed. "I didn't rape a girl in the woods."

"You tried to rape me."

"Shut up, you faggot."

"Don't call my son that," Dad yelled as he scrambled to his feet.

"Whoa there, cowboy." Jessie took a step back toward the body of the elk. The blood wasn't visible on the ground, though the arrow was still buried in the elk's neck.

"Don't do anything you'd regret," said Jessie.

There was breath steaming from the elk's nostrils.

"Jessie, no one is going to kill anyone," shouted Rick. "Put the gun down."

"I didn't rape no one. Tell 'em, Travis."

Travis didn't move, didn't look up.

"Travis, tell them!"

Vivian had never noticed how afraid Travis was of his dad. Of course he was afraid. Vivian wasn't the first person Jessie had done this to. The weight of all their eyes burned against her, except Dad's. Dad was watching the elk.

The ground stirred as the elk rose to his feet.

"I'll kill all of you fuckers if I have to." Spit flew from Jessie's lips. "In fact, it might be best if you killed your son first, Mike. Save you from the shame of him."

Dad lunged at Jessie.

A piercing, inhuman scream filled the clearing. Jessie flew up into the air, impaled on the horns of the young bull elk. His body thrashed, casting a red mist over the white snow. The crack of the .45 thundered over them. The elk whipped its head and tossed Jessie across the clearing. His body folded into a ball. The bull reared up and came down in front of her, bowing, blood dripping at Vivian's feet. She reached out and touched his muzzle. He chuffed, turned away, and headed down the mountain path into a twilight fog.

In the ranger station, she sat sipping poorly mixed hot cocoa and listened to the men lie.

They claimed that they'd thought the elk was dead and that Jessie was showing off. "It was an accident," Rick said. The rangers said there'd be an investigation, and they may have more questions. Vivian had answers, but doubted that anyone would ask, or if they did, whether they would listen.

Travis, wrapped in a blanket, was sitting across from Kyle at a ranger's desk. He hadn't said a word since they left the clearing and he wouldn't look at anyone. He still shook.

When the rangers were finished with the men, Dad sat down next to her. She offered him the remaining cocoa. It was no longer hot, but he cupped it in his hands and stared into the opaque liquid.

"I'm sorry," he said with his eyes closed. "I'm so, so, sorry, Will. I am so sorry. I just." He slumped over the cup.

She hugged him. He leaned into her and let go. She pulled him tighter and he was so small. She didn't know what to say other than, "It's okay." And even though that wasn't really right, it felt like a very small promise that it would be, one day.

Bernadette Marie Oliver is a graduate of the 2015 Class of Clarion Science Fiction and Fantasy Writers' Workshop, and received an MFA Creative Writing from Roosevelt University.

Bernie has taught fiction writing, screenwriting, literature, and composition; curated FeedBack, an experimental music concert series; ran a staged reading series for screenwriters; served as Assistant Artistic Director for the Tamale Hut Café Reading Series in North Riverside, IL; served on the Board of Directors of the University City Arts League in Philadelphia; and recently worked as a volunteer at the Lambda Archives of San Diego.

Stories in *Five on the Fifth, A cappella Zoo, Blood and Lullabies, Collective Fallout, Crack the Spine,* and *Up the Staircase Quarterly*. Follow at @bernadetteoliver.bsky.social

Corrupt the World with Drum[2]

Alicia Cole

I hear the drum beating.
What is it saying in the heartbeat of the world
other than look at the earth?
And the earth is there,
and the earth is always there.

I was conceived in Cades Cove
in the Smoky Mountains. In a tent.
Aren't we always in a tent?
The red tent, the biblical tent,
the tent from other books I was never taught
that are also holy. I was conceived
in a tent and God came down
where the deer graze and the cars move
slowly over the long roads where people graze
on McDonald's and peanuts and Coca Colas
and slowly roll through the park.

My parents rolled in the dark,
and I was conceived. My twin and I.
In Cades Cove. Perhaps this is why
I look at the earth and make a muddle of myself
wondering why people toss garbage
instead of making love and making children through love
and making children through the Bible
(or whatever holy book or unbook
or unBible or anything else, for I believe
in everything, including the Bible).
Make a muddle of myself and toss my hands
in my hair under my hat, for I am strong,

---

2 From a quote by Babatunde Olatunji

and weak, and do not understand how
to accept the ways of men
who toss and leave muddle on the ground.

Where will we go when we don't conceive
ourselves properly? Where will we go
when everything is overrun with the wrong
kind of strength?

I would like to find the place of my conception
and sit there and feel God
and draw power from that spot
and perhaps bless the earth that way
or at least teach how to bless the earth that way
by finding our place of being
and being there and showing others
our being there.

And thus sing. And thus beat two sticks
together. The way God is always beating
us together at the very beginning
when sperm meets egg, beating sticks
together and making dry dead things sing
to do what's needed on this dry earth
that is so in need of our blood's water.

Alicia Cole is a writer and artist in Huntsville, AL. She's the editor of Priestess & Hierophant Press. Her work has appeared in *Asimov's*, *Strange Horizons*, *Mythic Delirium*, and *Uncanny Magazine's Disabled People Destroy SciFi*, among other publications, and is forthcoming in *SageWoman* and *NILVX*. She's Asperger's, learning disabled, mentally ill, bisexual, genderfluid, and a practitioner of non-normative religions. She lives with her husband, five animals, and five plants. Her work has been a finalist for Best of the Net, won Honorable Mention in *Hermeneutic Chaos*' Jane Lumley Prize for Emerging Writers, and been selected as Longform's Fiction of the Week. She loves coffee, tattoos, animals, plants, and art.

Letters from Alouette Correctional Centre for Women

The Reverend Emilie Teresa Smith

August 9, 2018

I have paper! I have a pencil! I'm in jail! The world is sharply divided. There is a here and a not here, a yes and a no. Mostly the women in green, like me, are broken and hurt, of course. The women in uniforms are thoughtful and gentle, at least to me, at least for now. All is well. I sleep, eat, wonder, try to phone out, but can't make things work, so I settle and I wait.

Yesterday was like a strange dream.

"Guilty," said the judge, and then it all happened quickly, and then just as quickly stopped. Handcuffs, and down and away. Steve looks a glance of firmness and love as they take him away first. I get a glance of Patti and the others.

Cal and Gil seem sorry to do this. They can barely look at me. My organic blueberries go into the garbage. My wedding ring, so recently acquired, goes into a little safe baggie. My jacket goes—it has an attached strap that could be used in harmful ways. And then the waiting begins. The holding cell is in the bottom floor of the beautiful Arthur Erikson courthouse.

I sleep on the hard plastic bench, a sideways toilet roll is my pillow. I shake with cold. Gil checks on me, brings me an old red sweatshirt. It smells foul, but I take it with thanks. The yellow, shining cement bricks become Rosary markers and I pray: Lord Jesus Christ, Son of God, have mercy on me. Holy Mary, mother of God, Our Father, old way, new way. If I close my eyes and drift it goes to the old way, but I like the new one: Save me from the time of trial.

This is no trial, uncomfortable, inconvenient, but not that hard. Cold, clear, everything taken away, nothing to do. Pray, sing, sleep. My mind moves, slips into the border between dream and vision. A Holy Place of the great invisible. An Anarchic Vacation from the Law.

There is no clock or time, but the men come and go and peer into the window. I am cold even with the sweatshirt, so I get up and pace. That seems to be what one should do in jail. I try some of the salsa moves that Michael taught us before the wedding, but no. Not only do I have two left feet, I can't remember a single thing . . . but then joy! I remember the Swedish dancing from the winter! Step, lift, step, step. Step, step, step, step, turn, turn step, step. I figure out how to time the twirl so it misses the semi-wall that shields the smelly toilet, and the dip. I dance, sing, pray. The hours slide down into one another. Muffled, unrecognizable voices, distress, keys shaking. Time is measured by Gil's 15-minute footsteps, peering into the porthole, smiling, thumbs up, disappearing. He brings me lunch—a McDonald's chicken salad—and he's gone.

I dance and sing, I pace, I lie down again, I adjust my arms inside the jacket sweater, leaving the sleeves dangling. Desperation begins to settle, boredom, apprehension, loneliness, fear—but not really.

Maria Choc is on trial this day in Guatemala.

Edwin Espinal is in jail in Honduras.

How many thousands of Guatemalans were kidnapped, held, tortured, disappeared, murdered, mutilated? Was Beatriz even ever held in a jail? I sing a lament.

The expected graffiti is scratched into the door. True love and R.I.P. and a few foul declarations: Fxck thee cops. There all goofs. Girl Thugs. A couple of East Van Rules, and maybe my favourite: Tracy and Joseph . . . Best Friends Alwayz. These markings say: Here I am, here I was, I loved, I lost, I mattered. Into the days and years to come, forgotten, dead maybe, in jail, slivers of staying, remnants of saying I am. I pray for Tanya and Joseph, for Shorty, for Bubs.

At last Gil comes. He takes away the sweatshirt, and we're moving. Handcuffs and shackles this time, which cuff and rub and hurt my sockless feet. Into a van. All in our own hot boxes. Gleeful defiant men a few slots down. They yell, "Are you really a pastor, or is that a costume?" I forgot I was wearing my black shirt with a collar. "Ha! Ha! Hallelujah!" one man yells. I try and look around but can't see Steve anywhere. My ankles ache. And then we're off through the downtown streets, so strange through a little caged window, to the Main Street courthouse.

I shuffle awkwardly into the building, off come the cuffs. I stand hands against a wall, lift one foot, and another, off come the shackles, and into another cold holding cell where I see D., my first fellow prisoner. I am about to hear the first of many, many stories. These are not my stories to retell, but what I can say is that with everyone who shares with me, and many, many do—there is a common thread. Violence, sexual violence particularly, substance use, addictions, layered upon layer, from the very beginning of life, or at least memory. Beautiful girls, lovely women, every one.

D. paces a true jail pace, pounds on the door, anxious to leave. She got bail today and wants to get back to Alouette, maybe the people from the recovery house will wait for her and take her out. We have to get there before seven. Chains and shackles again and out to the van. D. and I share a tight bench in a cage. There's a woman with black hair sitting on the narrow slit of floor in the next cage over. "What's your name?" yells D. The other woman looks up, but shakes her head and looks down quickly. After 6pm now, we head out along Cordova. Hi St. James, hello Commercial Drive, Victoria, hello 1900 block, hello my darling, my house-family, Fritz, garden, bread, cheese, coffee, chocolate, figs and tomatoes and blackberries and the last raspberries and pillows and stuffies and books and clothes and photos of boys and Oscar, flowers and birds and spiderwebs strung across everything.

It is stinking hot and the woman in the cage beside us in distressed. She gets up, crouching, no one could stand. Highway One inches along. At last we stop and wait forever in a hot parking lot, waiting for another van, collecting prisoners to take home for the night. Our neighbour is ever more agitated until she is pounding and kicking at the door and walls. "I am dying! Help! I can't breathe!" D. tells her to shut up, but then somehow I am helping D. take off her green sweatshirt, separate from her green tee, it hangs over her cuffed hands. Our neighbour takes off her sweater too, but she can't undo the t-shirt, so it comes off too. She kicks again at the door, slumps, and is quiet.

I lean my head against the caged window between the two of us and shut my eyes, until I open them and look over. She's done the same thing at exactly the same time and suddenly we are looking into each other's eyes, both frozen, about four inches apart. We both start, surprised at such strange closeness, almost nakedness, human and woman and sad.

Who knows her great sadness. And mine? Wondering if we'll win or lose. The Judge, the Prosecutor, the Company, the Government, the Law. When is the law the foundation of our humanity and when does it serve only those most powerful, those rich enough to make the power work for them alone? How can we stop this destruction, this peril that seems so far away from this very moment, but is why I am here? Global warming and pipelines and bitumen. And me.

Suddenly the van jerks and moves and D. cheers. I am relieved too, longing for the what-ifs and unknowns to end, and to rest somewhere. Then—what? Wait? Where are we turning? D. peers through the narrow thick window, and now she's yelling and swearing, pounding in frustration. We turn to go over the big bridge, and down, down into Surrey. We'll never make it "home" before seven. We pull into another driveway, another jail, and inside, and wait. We are moved to another van, and getting in beside us come four young women, recently convicted, like me, exhausted, still high, dirty, worn and done. They stare and stare at me.

One young woman is fierce-eyed, shorn head, tattoos on her face and barefoot. D. says to me, "She's cursing us. Don't look at her." Obedient, I look down, but then we're driving back up through Surrey, and she throws herself at the window, head up to a small filtered screen up top. "My grandpa would want me to do this," she yells. "Are you a priest? Will you hear my confession?"

I'm too astonished to reply, and she starts to list things. I can't really hear her, the screen is too small, and the traffic too loud, but I hear some. Dear Lord, what to say, what to do? I know nothing about this young woman, not even her name, but I know she is reaching for that truth-star and I say what I've said many times before, though never in these circumstances:

"I don't know you. I know nothing about you, but this I know: No matter what you have done, no matter what has been done to you, you are a beloved daughter of God. You are loved. God holds you in the palm of his hand, and God treasures your heart." I yell through the grate that I can't say more. We sit in silence. Silence all around, or rather the steady roar of the van. It is less hot. The sun is setting and we are arriving home: The Alouette Correctional Centre for Women.

The shackles are rubbing a small sore on my shin, and the handcuffs are heavy. We are brought into yet another bright room to be processed yet again. The young women are spent and throw themselves on the hard bench as we are called out one by one. I go through the final process, am stripped of my own clothes and get green prison sweats. Everyone attending shakes their head. Who are they to say so to the judge, but this, to them is ridiculous. I have more allies, more friends.

I hear I am going to Alpha: the special secure unit. I shuffle down the long, nightmare hall with heavy locked doors on either side, and into the tiered unit. I am inside now.

Alpha in the secure zone is maximum but for the least troublesome—the immigration cases are here, they say. My ears perk up. But I'm too tired to notice much—an open area, and clanging stairs. I'm up to the second floor, a small cell, a bag of sheets and a towel, the door closes and locks and I sit and plan the night. I don't have a toothbrush or soap, so I make my bed and arrange a shirt over my face. The lights never turn out here. And the day is done. Two thin slits show the outside, a patch of yellow grass under the glare of blazing light, and the dark forest beyond.

The days stretch out down the way, but first there's the first night. Now everything is obviously gone. Industrial silence. And so, I turn in and examine myself.

My heart is pierced through with love, none of it earned by my goodness. It just is: Patti, my beloved boys, their girls, Oscar, the new little one coming, my family and my family-in-law, and my house family, my church, my brothers and sisters in Christ, my co-land defenders everywhere, especially in Latin America, and especially Guatemala, my doggie, the forest, the great sea, the looming mountains, and the wee sparrows. All these are my nest of prayer. And so, I weave them all around me, and sleep comes gently and carries me into the heart of God, where I spend the night free.

August 10, 2018

I wake up stiff on the board-hard mattress, and I stretch before opening my eyes. Outside it is that thin light that waits as dawn approaches over the trees. I no longer decide most things, so the things I do I cherish. Mostly what I have is me, and how I can be with everyone I meet.

I am so absolutely conscious of my privilege. I will be here for a few days, loved and carried by all that I have. I have no life to reconstruct from scratch when I leave, my traumas are not deep and lasting. So how can I mirror compassion without curiosity? Can I be open and vulnerable, reaching out with a measure of concern and confidence, in the flash moment of time that I will have here? No problem. I have done this before. I say a quick prayer and sing a little bit to warm up my heart. And I wait.

At seven the doors click unlocked, and a guard, H., comes by and turns a key, and I step out to the balcony, seeing for the first time others in green now stepping out. Two women are busy in the common area below, setting up plastic trays, and a breakfast is served: raisin bran with watery milk, a muffin, sweet, and two pieces of wonderbread. Coffee, a powdered creamer, four packs of sugar, a portion each of margarine, jam and peanut butter—oh and an apple. I'm eating quietly, politely, and slowly I say a few words and it happens. T.L. and J. start talking, I have delivered to me a story, and another. T.L. tells me some things, and her eyes narrow, and she asks me to pray with her, I think not quite believing I will. "Of course I will," I say. "We'll find a place and a time. I'm not going anywhere, at least for a few days."

J., in the meantime, is telling me how things work. Fill in this form for this, that form for that.

I'm looking at the soggy bread on my tray, and over by the phones I spy a toaster. Toasted is so better.

"Can I just go over and toast this?" I ask J. "Oh no," she says. "You have to fill in a form first!"

I look horrified, then she grins at me. We laugh. My first jail joke!

I give T.L. my muffin. "Really?" she asks. "You don't want it later?" "I'm good," I say.

E. comes by. I give her my sugar and whitener. "Jail candy!" she says. "Mix sugar, whitener, jam and p.b. Microwave for 30 seconds. Let harden. Eat."

Before we're shooed back to our cells, I find the book cart—and a book on dogs! Oh no, it's sentimental and inspirational. I slide it back. Next, I find a Bible—Yay! And then *Atonement* by Ian McEwen. Back in my cell I get lost in a world of child writers and big houses and real from another place—not here. Then I hear a call—Yoga! And we're clattering down the steps and through the door to the only outdoor space, a weird stuffy courtyard with a screen ceiling two floors above. But I can see that the sky is blue, and incongruously I'm lying on my back looking up, and then doing downward dog.

We have a jail meeting. I nod to everyone. I make a few more friends, there's some drama, some quiet, some promises, some pain.

The drama of me-not-being-able-to-phone begins. Deposit money in jail account. Done on arrival. Set up special phone voice recognition ID. Done. Try and call, no go. Oh. Must fill in form to transfer money from jail account to phone money. Do this. Must wait now until later. Okay. Sigh. Notice while rifling bored through the request forms that we have to ask specially for a visitor. Fill in a request for a visitor. Wait. Get a small plastic toothbrush and a cheap slip of hotel soap. Celebrate.

The regular rhythm of the day plods along. Now it is lunch, and then we are locked in for the afternoon. *Atonement* is seamless and transporting. Read, read, read. So desperately quiet and alone.

Then the guard, S., comes in—we're moving you. Right now. Hurry! Pack, sort, clothes/bed clothes. Wait, I'm leaving T.L. and we never got to pray. Can I say goodbye, guards? No. Okay. Rats. Out. Long hall, nightmare doors. Strip off the green clothes, switching to grey. I've been moved from secure Alpha to medium Cedar B.

Cedar B. The Canine Unit. You've got to be kidding me? Arf. Six dogs here, with 23 women. The 'girls' have finished their workday and they're lounging about—laughing. It is LOUD—jarring after the quiet of Alpha. Booming voices and roaring laughter. The small bungalow shakes. It is three in the afternoon. Still hot and sunny. August air—for the first time in almost two days I breathe, and there are birdies, and ants and dragon flies. And trees for 360 degrees, beautiful cedars and firs.

There are gardens, a memory area, with painted stones for the dead, and a labyrinth—no actually—a spiral. I come back after dinner and hop its painted tiles. And I stay out until almost 10.

Some of the girls call this Camp Cupcake, but it is a prison, of course. We can see the forest, but not go into its cool shade. And this day and the next, and the next, the stories spill out. I hear them and I brace: Mothers have died, and brothers, and boyfriends are in jail too, and children have been taken away, who knows where they are and worst of all, a child, a daughter who died. Drugs stab in and out of most stories. There is talk of lawyers and trials to come, and days and months and years to wait. And there is drama, and exhaustion and frustration, and lots of swearing. I am uncomfortable with some women—there are more than 40, on both sides of the Cedar bungalow—and there are the don't-give-a-shit ones, loud and sarcastic.

Pretty soon they know why I'm here—there's some amazement—that someone would more-or-less do this voluntarily, but then some nods of interest, and good job, and that A-Hole of a judge, and I look for a way to be still, show interest, compassion, welcome, with no prying, and I balance with escapes to quiet—relatively—and green.

Phone drama—I filled the request form, but it was done incorrectly in pencil—they wouldn't give me a pen—and that doesn't count. Damn it. I borrow a pen and fill in the form again. It should work tomorrow. Okay, I say.

In the meantime a guard, A., takes me to the library—looking for a replacement for *Atonement* which they wouldn't let me take from one side to another, and while I'm there she whispers "You did fill in the visitor request form? You have to fill it out and request it, before they can schedule a visit." "I have indeed," I reply. A. says under her breath, "I talked with her." A flash of sympathy, and then a sliver of her own story. She talks, and I nod and we smile furtively. Then she goes out. I follow. The flowers are singing: Patti is coming! Maybe, not sure, but when? Tomorrow is Friday.

I take my new book outside. The sun has set into the trees to the west. The raucous girls laugh on the steps. One women ignores everything and waters the lawns and the flowers and the flower pots with a rough determination. I write with my new glorious pen at a table, now shaded for the night. On the tops of the eastern trees the sun still lights up the branches. A hawk, a fat one, flies straight over, from east to west.

There was morning, and there was evening. The first day.

August 11, 2018

Friday morning, a work day. I'm on Hort. After breakfast I get new clothes and work boots. I follow my new roomie, B., out to the spiral. Together with two other women we weed, for hours in an ever-tightening path towards the centre. On my knees I pull weeds from the stepping tiles, leaving the hens and chicks, which bubble up, thick, prickle-less succulents that spread and grow everywhere. The two women I don't know are talking, loudly, well, one woman is talking, the other is listening, nodding, saying uh-uhum, and a few words of comfort and solace. Pluck, pluck, dig, and I can't help but hear another tale of horror. My heart contracts. It actually aches. The speaker leaves, and I say to the woman left, "Your voice sounds so nice as you listen." She nods, and ping! We see each other.

After break we move to the lavender patch. I sit harvesting in the shade, surrounded by purple, breathing in calm, peace. The bees and I take turns reaching for the flowers. I watch one take its time, and I wait for it to finish. Lavender saturates everything, my lap, my hands, my clothes, my hair, the scent stays for a while. We stack them, tray by tray in the greenhouse. B. warns me: "Don't even take one flower. You could get punished." Oh dear. I've already taken one small sprig and tucked it into my rib-squashing, chest-flattening bra. The contraband lavender pricks my skin guiltily. I don't have any intention of following this rule.

After lunch it's too hot to be outside, so I'm allowed into the empty library. I sort and stack and arrange in cool silence—the Dog books and the God books are all jumbled up on two long, low shelves—until it's time to rush back to Cedar and stand with B. outside our door. We are counted at 7am, 11am, 1pm, 4pm, 7pm and 10pm, standing like sentinels guarding our own cells.

I don't feel like going back to the library now, so I lay down for a while. But now there's nothing to do. I let a little bit of Patti-sad into my heart, just a small sliver of longing. I remember her singing—of course I do—and waving her hands, and holding me, and wondering why I do what I do, and loving me right through it. My boys too, Abel at the demo with his sign. Oscar. His wispy red-gold curls more precious than a million mountains of gold, die-for-him precious, give-the-whole-world-for-him precious. And the women here, and their children, and their love, and their longing. It makes me furious. I cry two tears, that's all for now, in frustration. Maybe Patti's coming today, this afternoon. Two extra tears for hope.

After a while I spring up and go to the pay phone—maybe it will work at last now. I follow the commands, punch in several series of numbers, say my name three times. The voice recognition ID fails. I go to a guard, can you check this out? "Oh, your voice ID has become invalid. Fill out a form (in pen) to request a reset. It should work by 3pm tomorrow."

The afternoon is hot and maybe will never end. I go outside and sit by the roses for a while. The roses surround the closed-up Eagle Hut. The women tell me that the elders used to come and smudge and drum, and mysteriously they no longer have these healing circles. But, why? It's impossible to get any clear news of any sort here but surely Indigenous spiritual care here should be a priority. S. finds me on the bench by the hut. "I always come here to pray," she says. "I wish the elders would still come. It used to help so much, you can feel it healing." There is a sad carved eagle outside guarding the way into the round building.

I head back inside, and coming around the corner of the bungalow I find a large group of women including A., the loudest-laughiest of them all. "Hey," she says. "Tell us more about why you are here." Deep breath.

"Well," I start, "the pipeline would bring really dirty oil from Alberta to a place in Burnaby where they plan to ship it over the ocean. There would be seven times as many oil tankers going through the water out to the sea. There could be an oil spill—and that would be the end of the orcas and the sea animals and fish and life along the coast. And the First Nations people there, the Tsleil-Waututh—they never gave their land away in the first place. There was no treaty or anything for their land, and they don't want the pipeline at all."

We enter into a robust talk about climate change and indigenous rights and reconciliation—many of the women I've met along this jail journey are First Nations. There are lots of nods and more right-ons, until one woman stands up and says, "I'm all for the pipeline."

"Hmmm," I say. "Tell me more."

"I'm from Alberta, and we need jobs," she says, looking defiant, if a bit nervous.

"I totally agree with you," I say. "About the jobs. Of course people need jobs." Her eyes are interested.

"My son's a carpenter," I go on. "He's been to the protests with a sign that says Carpenter for Sustainable Energy Projects. There's lots of jobs in making clean energy. More jobs for a long period of time. This pipeline will make some jobs, but mostly it is about a small group of people making a pile of money, and wrecking the earth."

The vigorous discussion continues until A. says, "Teach us to protest!" Uh-oh.

"Hmmm," I say again. "Well, what would you like to protest?"

"The awful food and the expensive extras we have to buy from the canteen."

"What do you think you could do?"

"Write letters." "Protest at the admin building." "Blockade the kitchen." "Go on a hunger strike!"

I smile and leave them to it, retiring again to read for a while before dinner. After about ten minutes I look out the window, and I see a huge crowd, shouting and gesticulating in front of the main building. Uh oh. Now I've done it. I sink down behind my book again.

D. comes into our room.

"What's happening out there?" I ask timidly.

"Oh, nothing," she says. "We're just getting our meds."

"Oh", I say, ever so slightly disappointed.

Dinnertime comes, and is gone in ten minutes. My roomie is watching crime shows on tv, so I go outside and read, and then wander and wander. I'm tamping down a circle in the grass. Up to ten feet from the fence allowed, and then around and back. I remember the circling polar bear, disgracefully held in a cramped and crumbling enclosure at the Stanley Park zoo. Thank heavens it's gone. Poor bear. Pace, pace, turn around, pace, pace went the creature, twenty-five feet where a thousand were required.

In the north, the sea ice is melting; further south the forests are burning. Over the thick green trees here to the west of the prison, Venus pops out shining.

August 12, 2018

Saturday morning. There is a thin haze over the pale sky. No work today, no lavender, no weeding, no hours in the cool library. And no breakfast! "Brunch" is at 10. One hard-boiled egg, one slice of bacon, wonderbread. The gals invite me to coffee—real coffee, strong, made from their canteen stash. The morning is long and drawn out. D. and I go to the gym for a bit. Huff, puff, step, pull. The minutes go slow.

And then I hear there's a Catholic Mass. Well, I've always been ecumenical, and I hope the priest is too, because of course I'm going. G. and I head over. G. is older, like me, and from a community up the Fraser River. She's hoping her brothers will put up some salmon for her for the winter. Some others hear we're going to Mass and come along. Father M. and the three volunteers who come with him look up in surprise. So many people. The small circle is full. And so we pray.

How could I, how could anyone come as a Christian to prison but as a penitent? Any wrongs by the women in grey were first wrongs done to them. In what way did the State, the Church fuck up first? Grabbing the land, out-lawing the Potlach, Indian Residential Schools, smallpox by intent or by accident, poisoning the waters, ripping down the trees, killing the buffalo, the caribou, the salmon, alcohol, poverty, derision, soul-crushing, body-crushing violence of every kind. And then to try to reform these women? These lovely, precious, fierce women—once girls, born perfect. T.L. back in Alpha said, "I'm so angry, so fucking angry at everyone."

Father M. is kind and encouraging, and we sing loudly, though I'm not sure that much we say and sing really makes sense here. But the beauty of the Christian Mass is that it doesn't matter at all who says the words. And the words themselves carry our faith, through the distortions and confusions and the sins, the horrendous sins, of a fallen church.

"This poor soul cried, and was heard by the LORD, and was

saved from every trouble." Jesus came for those abandoned, crushed, forgotten, expelled. To restore those who had been crucified by a greedy, violent world. Love embodied for you, and for you, and for me.

Fr. M. tugs a bit at his collar, the earnest women with him smile helpfully. The vessels of his communion set shine brilliantly and clean.

And somehow we take and taste and see that the Lord is good. I sit down in silence.

I'm burning angry, too. Ready still to stand with land defenders everywhere, to turn over every table of the truly guilty. Carving and crapping all over this holy earth. They must be stopped.

G. and I and the others trip out again into the blasting sunshine. It's lunchtime and then wait time. Will Patti come, did she even get the message?

I go to the phone one last time to see if I can make the damn thing work. Nope. I check with the guard yet again. She looks on the computer. "Oh, no. You are getting out tomorrow. Your phone money has been transferred back into your trust fund." Sigh. Then the guard whispers to me, "Don't go far. She's coming at 2:45."

One hour from now! The longest hour of my life begins. Sixty seconds times 60 minutes. That's 3600 seconds. I count slowly. My stomach hurts. I don't believe anything. I've forgotten everything anyway. I give up. Who cares?

I lie on my bed and feel guilty. Not many visits happen for these women, and I've been here for just a flash of time. I'm going home tomorrow. Who am I to silently whine? I try to kill every emotion. And at last the guard comes for me. We walk over to the main building, down the nightmare hall of doors.

I wait outside the door of visiting room number one. Will I be able to hug her at least, a small kiss? Will we sit at a table, in a lounge? I go up the narrow stairs, open the door . . . shock. We are in real prison mode. A chair in a small, enclosed glass box, with a desk, facing an identical box with the same. A small circle-screen between us.

But never mind—there she is. My love. And I can't believe my eyes: she's wearing her wedding jacket. Nothing could have been better. Patti in that jacket, with her ring still on, and everything is restored in me. Jail is meant to kill the spirit, and in a small way mine had been suffering, until now.

We have the strangest conversation of our lives. Small talk, a few stories. How is the dog?

"I'm getting out tomorrow, 8:30 am," I say!

"Tomorrow! Damn, I'm working. I'll figure it out."

She brought chocolate (can't have it) and a printout of all the messages she'd been receiving. Can't have that either.

"Should I read them?"

"No, I can't stand it."

"Well, I'm bringing a U-Haul of love, support and prayers."

"I know you are." All I can think of is T.L. and S. and D. and G. and everyone.

And before we can end the awful, precious visit, the guard comes. Patti goes first. I'm left standing in the echo chamber of the stairwell. And what else should I do, but sing?

Back in the yard, I wander again. Everything is weird. Calm. Until A. and R. get into a water fight. A phalanx of guards swoops down, and I walk around the side to look at the lavender that's left to be clipped on Monday. Not by me.

My last ten-minute supper. Then it's Saturday night bingo! We wander over to the gym. There's lots of rules, but we settle in at last. We have time for nine rounds, and I win the eighth! I hand my winnings ($2) over to the elder, G. We hurry through the ninth game to be back and ready for the 7 pm count. I'm finally starting to get the hang of this.

What to do now? I feel like there's nothing I can say that will heal or help anything at this point. I hang around and admire beautiful beading and lovely crochet blankets. If I were only here longer. "I like the rainbow unicorn one," I say, to the woman beading Snoopy.

We talk a bit more about the people making a stand up on Burnaby Mountain.

"There will be more women coming," I tell them. "I'll tell them how nice you all are."

I decide to make the rounds of the grounds one last time, and say goodbye to the plants and the dragonflies. I stop to smell the smallest rose outside the boarded-up Eagle Hut. I sit on the grass.

S. finds me here, and I don't really want to talk much more, but I can listen. "I used to cry right here a whole lot," she says. "After my son was murdered. He was four years old." I sit and hold that pain in my lap for a while. She's so used to telling the story. I know it must still hurt, but she smiles at me. Generous and gracious and beautiful.

Others come around the Hut. One woman cuts the tiny rose and hands it to S. who puts it in her golden hair. I'm sure that's against the rules, but I'm sure they know that too. Later on, as we walk together, all of us, back to the bungalow, the rose is invisible.

In bed by 9:30, I say goodnight to sweet D. And I sleep like a log until 6 the next morning. We're allowed out to go to the bathroom, but I quickly search for some coloured pencil crayons and markers I saw yesterday. All put away, except a green highlighter. I go back into the room and in the penumbra of the early morning in cell 25, Cedar B, I write out a prayer in blue ink and green highlighter to the women:

To My New Friends On Cedar
May the Lord bless you and keep you.
May the Lord make His face to shine upon you.
May the Lord be gracious to you, and grant you peace.
Love,
Emilie

And by 8:30 on the dot, after a pile of paperwork, and getting my phone money back plus $2.00 for working one day, I stand at the great metal gate, while the guard shouts: "Smith for release!"

Outside I see Lini, my dearest sister-in-law. She has brought tea and granola and yogurt and fruit. Of all the people on earth, I think she's the one I am happiest to see right then. I flail and dig until I find it—the little plastic bag with my wedding ring. Deep breath. I put it back on.

We slowly make our way back home, but first drive up that Holy Mountain, to greet the sacred fire, to say a prayer with those still standing there.

Emilie Teresa Smith is an Argentine-born Canadian Anglican priest, writer and theologian. Since 1984 she has walked with a profound commitment to the people of Guatemala. In 2012 she was elected co-president of the historic Oscar Romero International Liberation Theology Network (SICSAL). Since then she has visited every region of Latin America and the Caribbean, and has been privileged to come alongside numerous community struggles for the protection of sacred land and water. emilie@madlovefortheworld.com

Test Prints for #ExtinctionRebellion

#BODYPOLITIC

test prints of eyes for bodypolitic, anarchy bike borrowed from Internet, and the Symbol which I went on to start using on activist outfits ,,,, crossover period

I made this block kinda by mistake, then it kinda became a #prototype, then I was like we need to print thousands so I started the #silkscreen thing : : : Making a block kinda crystallizes things

#BODYPOLITIC is 2 humans, Tottyfuckshame and Milesinfinity8, making a creative response to the urgent times we find ourselves in. Working to encourage and facilitate others in a movement for positive resistance.